CarbSmart
PRESS

FAT FAST
COOKBOOK

50 Easy Recipes To Jump Start Your Low Carb Weight Loss

DANA CARPENDER
AMY DUNGAN & REBECCA LATHAM

A Division of *CarbSmart*, Inc.
http://www.CarbSmart.com

CarbSmart Press
CarbSmart, Inc.
P.O. Box 635,
Las Vegas, NV 89125-0635

Photography Copyright © 2013 by Amy Dungan & Jeff Guyer

Front cover design by Azure Zebra Productions.

Interior page design by John W. Furkin – Prospect House Designs.

CarbSmart® is a registered trademark of *CarbSmart, Inc.*

For information about special discounts on bulk purchases,
please contact CarbSmart, Inc. at customerservice@carbsmart.com.

DISCLOSURE: This document contains links to external websites that may provide financial benefits to the publisher, the authors, and/or CarbSmart, Inc. from click-through purchases.

www.fatfastrecipes.com/resources

Throughout this cookbook, you will see underlined text (example: Fat Fast Cookbook). These are references to additional resources on the Internet that provide more information about the the underlined text. You will find all of these references and their links at www.fatfastrecipes.com/resources.

ISBN 978-0-9704931-2-5

Version 1.04 Paperback

"I am really impressed with the recipes in this book. Dana & Co. did a great job. The recipes are fun, innovative, varied and easy. If one must do the fat fast, this book is a blessing."

JACQUELINE EBERSTEIN, R.N.

Controlled Carbohydrate Nutrition, co-author of Atkins Diabetes Revolution.

"Are you ready to burn some fat? A Fat Fast is an effective way to start the fire. Dana Carpender and the CarbSmart team have cooked up some really tasty tidbits to keep hunger at bay while you rev up your metabolism with the magic of nutritional ketosis. You might think eating 1,000 calories a day, with 90% of them from fat, would require a lot of discipline. You may even doubt that you could do it. This book will change your mind. The authors show you how to eat a rich and varied diet while eating in a way that lets you access your stored fat for energy. These are recipes you will continue to use long after you have reached your ideal weight. Who would have guessed you could lose weight eating like this?"

JUDY BARNES BAKER

Author of Nourished: A Cookbook for Health, Weight Loss, and Metabolic Balance and Carb Wars: Sugar is the New Fat.

"Looking to ditch the junk in your trunk, thin your thighs, and whittle your middle? This comprehensive guide not only shares why everything you thought you knew about fat-fasting was wrong, readers will glean extensive information, recipes and pictures so sexy you'll want to dress them in fishnets and spank their little bottoms. This book is a must-read for moving the scale in the right direction."

JAMIE VANEATON,

Your Lighter Side

Dedication

Everyone I know following a low-carbohydrate diet hits a plateau. Everyone. For some people, the weight-loss stall lasts for a few days and for some it lasts for a few months. The last thing I want is for anyone to give up on the low-carb lifestyle because of these stalls.

This book is dedicated to everyone who wants to break a low-carb stall and continue to succeed on a low-carb diet. These recipes are written for you.

This cookbook is also dedicated to Marcy Guyer who has worked with me for many, many years and who works very hard behind the scenes at CarbSmart to keep our business running.

Andrew S. DiMino
Publisher, President, and Founder
CarbSmart, Inc.

Contents

What is the Fat Fast
& Why Do We Do It?

by Dana Carpender

Everything You Know Is Wrong

For decades we have been told that fat makes us fat. After all, the logic goes, since fats have nine calories per gram, while proteins and carbs have four calories per gram, if we slash the fat from our diets, we'll be able to eat the same or an even greater volume of food and lose weight. After all, a calorie is a calorie is a calorie.

Right?

W R O N G . Prepare to have your mind blown.

What is a Fat Fast?

A Fat Fast is a diet in which a) caloric intake (joules, if you're in that part of the world) is strictly limited, and b) the vast majority of those calories - ideally 90% - come from fat. In _Dr. Atkins' New Diet Revolution,_ Dr. Robert C. Atkins recommended using a Fat Fast of 1,000 calories per day, 90% of them from fat, to break through metabolic resistance to weight loss.

What kind of crazy idea is that?!

A really brilliant crazy idea, and one backed up by research.

For over 30 years, we have been told that all that matters is calories-in versus calories-out; if we wish to lose weight, limiting calories is all that matters, not where those calories come from. That's why we have **100 calorie packs** and ads for everything from yogurt to breakfast cereal to soup that tout, not how nutritious they are, but how few calories they contain. But is the calorie theory correct?

There's little doubt that most people will lose weight if they restrict calories sufficiently, regardless of the source of those calories. If you ate just 200 calories per day of Moon Pies, you would very likely lose weight. Also your energy, your health, your muscle mass, and possibly your hair. But hey, you'd lose weight.

But will you lose an equal amount of weight with the same degree of caloric restriction, regardless of the source? Will the same percentage of pounds lost come from your stored fat mass, rather than your lean body mass? Or does the kind of calories you eat make a difference in how much fat you burn?

I assume that you've guessed by now that it does, or I wouldn't be writing this. How big a difference? A really, really big difference. Dig this:

In 1956, a groundbreaking study appeared in the highly respected medical journal *The Lancet*. Two British researchers, Prof. Alan Kekwick and Dr. Gaston L. S. Pawan, decided to look at this question of whether the type of calories consumed affected fat burning. A few years earlier, Dr. Alfred Pennington published an article in the *Journal of Clinical Nutrition* regarding his experience treating obesity with a calorically unrestricted ketogenic diet. Pennington asserted that his patients did not experience the drop in basal metabolic rate that usually accompanies caloric restriction, because **ketosis** allowed them to access their stored body fat, giving them all the energy - the calories - they needed to maintain the higher metabolic rate. *(Ketosis is a physiological state where, because you're not feeding it glucose - carbs - your body is running on fatty acids (fat burning, yay!), and a by-product of fat burning called **ketone bodies**, or ketones for short. Most of your body's tissues can run on fatty acids, but some, especially the brain, cannot, but can burn ketones just fine.)* Kekwick and Pawan wanted to expand on this information.

Here's what they did: They put obese subjects on low-calorie, *balanced* diets, at levels of 2,000, 1,500, 1,000, or 500 calories per day. Each patient stayed on each version of the diet for seven to nine days. You will be unsurprised to know that the fewer calories they ate, the more weight they lost.

Next, Kekwick and Pawan put obese subjects on one of four different diets. The diets all had the same calorie count - 1,000 calories per day - but the *composition of those calories* varied: 1,000 calories of a mixed or *balanced* diet, 1,000 calories with 90% from carbohydrate, 1,000 calories with 90% from protein, or 1,000 calories with 90% from fat. If it were true that a calorie is a calorie is a calorie, then patients should have lost roughly the same amount of weight on all four diets. **Did they?**

No. Indeed, on the high-carbohydrate diet the patients actually *gained* a little weight, overall - on just 1,000 calories per day. They lost some weight on 1,000 calories per day of a balanced diet, and even more on 1,000 calories per day with 90% from protein. But overwhelmingly, patients lost the most weight on 1,000 calories per day when 90% of those calories came from fat. Kekwick and Pawan concluded, *So different were the rates of weight-loss on these isocaloric diets that the composition of the diet appeared to outweigh in importance the intake of calories.*

Finally, Kekwick and Pawan determined that a group of patients could maintain their weight on 2,000 calories per day of a mixed or **balanced** diet. Then they put them on a diet of protein and fat, but very little carbohydrate. They found that their patients could consistently lose weight on 2,600 calories per day so long as carbohydrate was sharply restricted. This was one of the early pieces of research establishing a standard low-carb, Atkins-style diet for long term weight loss and maintenance.

In the 1960s, Dr. Frederick Benoit, working at Oakland Naval Hospital, put seven obese men on a total fast for ten days. They lost an average of 21 pounds each, which sounds great - but it turned out that 14 of those pounds were lean body mass. The subjects were losing far more muscle than fat. Bad ju-ju. Benoit then put the same men on 1,000 calories per day, with 90% of those calories from fat. If a calorie really is a calorie, they should have lost less weight, and certainly less fat, than they did eating nothing at all.

But they didn't. They lost less weight, yes - an average of 14 pounds in ten days. But only 0.5 pounds of that weight, on average, came from lean body mass. Benoit's subjects had lost **nearly twice as much fat** eating 1,000 calories per day as they had eating nothing at all - and they'd protected their muscle mass in the process.

I trust the potential is clear.

How I Got Interested In This

As I write this, I have been eating a low-carbohydrate diet for 17 years - more than 30% of my life. It has been hugely beneficial to me, and helped me go from a size 20 to a size 12. However, like so many low-carbers, I reached a plateau - my weight was staying off, but I was still a little bigger than I wanted to be.

I had read about Fat Fasting in _Dr. Atkins' New Diet Revolution,_ and had also seen the work of Kekwick and Pawan, Benoit, and Pennington. It had been in the back of my mind that I needed to try it sometime, I just hadn't gotten around to it.

Suddenly I needed to drop ten pounds, fast, before shooting a television pilot. I tried the Fat Fast, lost a pound a day, felt fine doing it - even had _a great weight-lifting workout_ - and improved my blood sugar readings in the bargain. I was sold.

It's funny how ideas seem to reach a critical mass, and suddenly take hold. In the past year, several friends of mine, long-time low-carbers, have tried eating a higher percentage of fat, with excellent results. It seems that the time has come.

What About All That Fat?
And Cholesterol!
Won't It Kill Me?

In a word: No.

First of all, if you've been eating the Standard American Diet, you won't actually be getting much more fat than you are already eating. The average American gets 45% of his or her calories from fat. If you're eating around 2,000 calories per day - a not-unlikely number - then cutting back to 1,000 calories per day, 90% from fat, will result in your eating exactly as much fat as you've been eating all along. You're not increasing fat. You're just cutting out the other stuff.

If you've been eating an Atkins-style low-carb diet all along, you may well eat *less* total fat on a Fat Fast, for the simple reason that you'll be eating less, period.

Some of you are thinking, ***Shouldn't I eat healthful fats?*** Yes, you should - but you may be thinking of the wrong fats. Animal fats are just fine on a Fat Fast - and in general - and so are butter, cream, and cream cheese. It's polyunsaturated vegetable oils, like soy oil and safflower oil, that you must avoid, along with hydrogenated vegetable oils, aka ***trans fats.***

Secondly, the whole ***saturated-fat-causes-heart-disease*** hypothesis has been largely discredited. According to the World Health Organization in 2010, ***Intake of SFA [saturated fatty acids] was not significantly associated with CHD (coronary heart disease) mortality... SFA intake was not significantly associated with CHD events (e.g., heart attacks).*** In the same year, *The American Journal of Clinical Nutrition* published a meta-analysis of 21 studies that looked at the effects of saturated fat consumption on coronary artery disease. The conclusion?

A meta-analysis of prospective epidemiologic studies showed that there is no significant evidence for concluding that dietary saturated fat is associated with an increased risk of CHD or CVD (coronary vascular disease).

A Great, Big, Huge Caution: DO NOT IGNORE

If you are a diabetic and taking any form of blood-sugar-lowering medication, especially insulin, DO NOT UNDERTAKE a Fat Fast WITHOUT MEDICAL SUPERVISION. Why? Because your blood sugar will drop so fast, your medication will need drastic adjustment within 24 hours or less. Your dosages of insulin and other hypoglycemic medications are predicated on your usual intake of carbohydrate. If you suddenly stop eating carbs, those dosages will be way, way too high.

Dr. Eric Westman, one of the country's premier researchers into low-carbohydrate nutrition, has worked extensively with diabetics. He cuts their insulin and other hypoglycemic medications in half on Day One of eating 20 grams per day or fewer of carbohydrate. They are told to monitor their blood sugar very closely, and medication is adjusted accordingly. Just about everyone has to reduce medication over time, and most need no medication at all if obesity was the cause of the diabetes.

However, YOU DO NOT WANT TO DO THIS UNSUPERVISED. Insulin shock can be fatal.
Do not screw around.

We (the publisher, the authors, and CarbSmart, Inc.) recommend you find a doctor who is hip to carbohydrate restriction for diabetes control, and get on a standard low-carb diet - Atkins, Protein Power, or the like - with that doctor's help. Read Dr. Bernstein's Diabetes Solution and the Atkins Diabetes Revolution to get a handle on the situation. Once your body has adjusted to carbohydrate restriction and your doctor has adjusted your medication accordingly, then you can consider trying a Fat Fast if you're not losing weight, or if you hit a plateau - but we still recommend you have a doctor's supervision.

This caution applies to anyone on blood-sugar-lowering meds for any reason, by the way - for instance, for polycystic ovarian syndrome (PCOS) or non-alcoholic fatty liver disease - and also to those who have been diagnosed as seriously hypoglycemic.

A Far Less Dire Caution

We are assuming that most people reading this are already on a low carbohydrate diet. If, instead, you have been eating American Standard (full of junk), or a low fat/high carbohydrate diet, whether of processed food or whole grains and beans, you have trained your body to run on glucose rather than fat. That can be changed, but it takes a transition period. Your body takes a few days to a few weeks to get with the program and create the enzymes necessary to burn fat for fuel instead of glucose. Because of this, going straight to a Fat Fast from a diet rich in carbohydrate will very likely make you feel awful for a few days - your body simply won't know where to get energy. We very much recommend that you go on a standard low carbohydrate diet first - we're big fans of <u>The New Atkins For a New You</u>, <u>Dr. Atkins' New Diet Revolution</u>, and <u>Protein Power</u>. Any of these very similar plans will give you an easier transition than jumping straight to the Fat Fast. Indeed, you may well find they're all you need to lose weight and improve your health.

Isn't Ketosis Dangerous?

No.

The confusion about ketosis comes because Type 1 diabetics have to be careful about ketoacidosis. Wikipedia (Some scoff at Wikipedia, but it's been shown to be on a par with the Encyclopedia Britannica for accuracy, and it's updated far more often) defines <u>ketoacidosis</u> as a pathological metabolic state marked by extreme and uncontrolled ketosis. This causes extremely high ketone levels, combined with very high blood sugar and acid accumulating in the blood. Again from Wikipedia, In healthy individuals this normally does not occur because the pancreas produces insulin in response to rising ketone/blood glucose concentration. In other words, this doesn't happen simply from carbohydrate restriction. If you have a functioning pancreas, you can't go into runaway ketosis. If you're making more ketones than your body is happy with, it will convert a little protein to glucose, release a little insulin, and bring your ketone levels down a bit.

The Benefits of Nutritional Ketosis

Dietary ketosis or nutritional ketosis appears to have numerous benefits. In particular, it provides energy while sparing muscle tissue. This would have been vital for our hunter-gatherer ancestors, who might well have to go out to hunt and gather on an empty stomach. In our modern age, ketogenic diets have long been used to treat epilepsy, and are now showing promise for *treating cancer* and *Alzheimer's*. And despite years of dire warnings about kidney damage, *recent mouse studies show a ketogenic diet reversing diabetic kidney damage*.

(There is a modestly increased rate of kidney stones among children on a severely limited ketogenic diet for seizure control. This apparently happens because liquids are restricted to allow ketones to build up in the blood. Liberalizing fluids generally solves the problem. So drink plenty of fluids.)

> Here's what *The Journal of the International Society of Sports Nutrition* has to say about ketones:
>
> During very low carbohydrate intake, the regulated and controlled production of ketone bodies causes a harmless physiological state known as dietary ketosis. Ketone bodies flow from the liver to extra-hepatic tissues (e.g., brain) for use as a fuel; this spares glucose metabolism via a mechanism similar to the sparing of glucose by oxidation of fatty acids as an alternative fuel. In comparison with glucose, the ketone bodies are actually a very good respiratory fuel. *Indeed, there is no clear requirement for dietary carbohydrates for human adults. Interestingly, the effects of ketone body metabolism suggest that mild ketosis may offer therapeutic potential in a variety of different common and rare disease states.* (Emphasis mine.)

Dr. Lubert Stryer, Professor of Biochemistry at Stanford University and the author of a biochemistry textbook used in many medical schools, says ketones are normal fuels of respiration and are quantitatively important as sources of energy. (In this usage, respiration doesn't mean breathing, but rather cellular respiration, the basic processes involved in creating energy within the cells.) Indeed, heart muscle, and the renal cortex [kidney] use [ketones] in preference to glucose.

Another biochemistry text, this one by Drs. Donald and Judith Voet, says that ketones serve as important metabolic fuels for many peripheral tissues, particularly heart and skeletal muscle.

Ketogenic diets similar to the Fat Fast, only without caloric restriction, have been used successfully for decades to treat epilepsy, and a 2006 article in the journal Behavioral Pharmacology states, there is evidence from uncontrolled clinical trials and studies in animal models that the ketogenic diet can provide symptomatic and disease-modifying activity in a broad range of neurodegenerative disorders including Alzheimer's disease and Parkinson's disease, and may also be protective in traumatic brain injury and stroke.

(The same article includes the information that The ketogenic diet may also protect against various forms of cell death.)

Sounds encouraging to me.

Because cancer cells are glucose-dependent, ketogenic diets are also being studied for cancer treatment.

Finally, here's the <u>abstract</u> from an article titled Ketogenic diets: additional benefits to the weight loss and unfounded secondary effects:

It is also necessary to emphasize that as well as the weight loss, ketogenic diets are healthier because they promote a non-atherogenic lipid profile, lower blood pressure and diminish resistance to insulin with an improvement in blood levels of glucose and insulin. Such diets also have anti-neoplastic (anti-cancer) benefits, do not alter renal or liver functions, do not produce metabolic acidosis by Ketosis, have many neurological benefits in the central nervous system, do not produce osteoporosis and could increase the performance in aerobic sports.

Ketones are your friend.

Fat Fast Game Rules

Let's cut to the chase: How to do this?

I'll be honest: Because fat is very high calorie, 1,000 calories per day, 90% of them from fat, is not a lot of food. You won't be eating meals. Instead, you'll be having four to five small *feedings* per day, about two to four hours apart - a cup of coffee with heavy cream for breakfast, an ounce of macadamia nuts three hours later, then in a few hours, a bowl of buttered shirataki noodles, and a couple of hours after that, perhaps a serving of low-carbohydrate vegetables in a high-fat sauce.

Here are the *game rules:*

Aim for 1,000 calories per day, with 90% of those calories coming from fat. Do not exceed 1,200 calories per day, or eat less than 80% of calories from fat.

Divide those calories among four to five *feedings* per day, each of about 200 to 250 calories. Space these out so that you're eating a little something every three to four hours.

Other than the high-fat, portion-controlled beverage recipes in this book - which count as *feedings* - drink zero-calorie beverages: water, tea, coffee, sparkling water. I cannot recommend that you consume much diet soda; there's too much evidence that it can stall weight loss and make you hungry.

If you eat something a bit low in fat, deliberately make up for it with something quite high in fat at your next feeding.

I regret to tell you that alcohol is right out. Sorry. You might try some of the relaxant herbal teas on the market; your local health food store should have a selection.

Take a good, strong multi-vitamin every day. You should be doing this anyway.

Keep track. There are good nutrition-counter apps available inexpensively, though they're likely to encourage you to eat low-fat. Ignore that part, just track your calorie count and percentages. Online, FitDay.com has a free nutrition tracker program I've used to good effect. I also have the free Calorie Counter & Diet Tracker app by MyFitnessPal on my iPhone. The problem with these apps is you'll need to enter ingredients one by one.

At the very least, keep track of your calories. If you balance the lower fat feedings with higher fat ones, the fat percentage should take care of itself.

Can You Give Me a Sample Menu?

Menu isn't really the right word, since it suggests more than one dish at a time. You won't be doing that on a Fat Fast. You'll be eating *only* a handful of nuts, or a cup of coffee with cream, or a couple of stuffed mushrooms, or a salad - just one food - at a time. You'll then wait a few hours, until actual, physical hunger sets in, and eat another dish.

A daily menu might look like this:

7 am: *Caramel Coffee* pg. 91 (210 calories, 22 grams fat, 92.4% fat)

10 am: ¼ cup *Curried Pecans* pg. 77 (235 calories, 24 grams fat, 87.6% fat)

1 pm: *Sweet 'n' Tangy Macaroni Salad* pg. 87 (223 calories, 25 grams fat, 93.8% fat)

4 pm: *Spinach Salad* pg. 72 (215 calories, 21 grams fat, 85.9% fat)

7 pm: 1 cup *Curried Coconut Cream of Chicken Soup* pg. 63
        (217 calories, 21 grams fat, 83.8% fat)

This comes to 1,100 calories. Calculating the exact fat percentage would be complex and tedious (and frankly, I'm not certain how to do it). However, you can be sure that it's above 85% of calories - well within our Fat Fast parameters.

But Won't I Be Starving?

Very likely not. Within a day or two, Fat Fasting will induce a state of deep nutritional ketosis - in other words, your body will shift from running on glucose (sugar) to running on fat and ketones. The vast majority of the tissues in your body can run happily on fat and ketones, especially your brain. If you've been eating a low-carb diet, you should have no hitch. If you've never slashed carbs before, you may have a day or two of feeling tired and groggy until your body remembers how to run on the fat/ketone fuel mix instead of on the glucose you've been feeding it. (However, if you haven't tried a low-carb diet, really, good old Atkins is the place to start, rather than this fairly radical protocol. Read *Dr. Atkins' New Diet Revolution* or *The New Atkins For a New You*, and get going!)

Here's the cool thing: Ketones have a profound appetite-suppressant effect. You may be mildly hungry the first day or two, but after that you should be fine. Just space your feedings out, eating only when you feel physically hungry.

I'm not uncomfortably hungry when I Fat Fast. Harder, is getting over the tendency to eat just to eat - grab a handful of something as I'm walking through the kitchen, or sit down to dinner because the clock says it's time. Most of us eat unconsciously, and there's no room for that on a Fat Fast. After a day or two, though, I'm so un-hungry that even this doesn't bother me much.

The Hardest Part

Honestly, the hardest part of Fat Fasting is getting up to 90% of calories per day from fat. Unless you like to eat straight butter, or can afford to eat nothing but macadamia nuts, it's hard. It's also hard to hit that 1,000 calorie mark exactly.

I have found that so long as I stay above 80% calories from fat, and under 1,200 calories per day, I lose weight like crazy, and am in a deep, appetite-suppressing ketosis. I'm guessing those numbers will work for you, too. After all, Kekwick and Pawan and Benoit's subjects had a dietary ward's kitchen making and measuring all their food for them. We're doing this at home, and are unlikely to be quite so precise. Shoot for the 90% fat/1,000 calorie mark, but if you find you've gotten to, say, 84% fat and 1,142 calories, no harm, no foul.

Dr. Atkins recommended a Fat Fast of five *feedings* per day, each with 200 calories. I find that unnecessarily rigid. The recipes in this book are designed to have 200 to 250 calories per serving - a few a little higher or lower - with 80% or more of those calories from fat. If you choose a recipe with 80% fat, balance it with higher fat feedings during the same day.

Unlike most cookbooks, this one is not arranged with a beverage chapter, an appetizer chapter, salads, soups, etc. Instead, I have grouped the recipes by fat content. This makes it easier to shoot for that 85 to 90% mark. If you have a recipe from the first chapter early in the day, have one from the last chapter later on. Conversely, if you have, say, **Keto Coffee** (*pg. 90)* at 95% fat, for breakfast, you can afford to have one of the lower-fat dishes later on.

Portion Control Is Essential

Remember that Fat Fasting isn't just about eating a very high-fat diet, it's also about caloric restriction. Because fat is so high in calories, it is easy to blow past the caloric limit. So long as you are Fat Fasting for quick weight loss, you should strictly observe the portions listed in the recipes. Many of the recipes make only one serving, so you don't have to worry about dividing a recipe into equal portions. Others make multiple servings. You'll need to be scrupulously honest with yourself when dividing them up.

If you've purchased this book because you're maintaining deep nutritional ketosis for sports performance, long-term weight loss, or therapeutic reasons, and want ideas for increasing your fat intake, portion control becomes less important.

Fiber and Water

Because a Fat Fast is calorie-restricted, and because fat is high in calories, portions can be quite small. For example, a portion of macadamia nuts is just ¼ cup. I find those nuts will keep me sated for a few hours, but they're not a satisfyingly big portion if I really feel like a meal.

If you crave a good-sized portion of food on a Fat Fast, your two best friends are fiber and water. Because they have neither usable calories nor carbs, these two items are free, or darned close to it. Add fat, and you get a dish that derives the vast majority of its calories from fat.

What foods can you use this way? Broth is mostly water, so soups made from broth plus fat, generally heavy cream or coconut milk, are good choices. Similarly, you'll find some high-fat coffee drinks in this book.

Very low-carb vegetables are largely a combination of fiber and water; add olive oil to make a salad, or butter, coconut oil, or other fat to sauté. Shirataki noodles, too, are pretty much a fiber-and-water blend, and can be used to make a satisfying portion. When I'm really hungry, I'll make a Fat Fast cream soup and serve it as a sauce over shirataki noodles.

Keep fiber and water in mind as you create your own Fat Fast recipes.

More About Fiber

I've had a few queries from people wondering how they can get enough fiber on a Fat Fast. Using the fiber-and-water strategy will help. If you like, you can also take a sugar-free fiber supplement, but I really don't think you will need to. First of all, I'm unconvinced that fiber, in and of itself, has a nutritional benefit. I think its good reputation comes from the fact that fiber-conscious folks tend to eat more vegetables and less junk food in general than people who aren't paying attention. Too, since fiber displaces some digestible carbohydrate, it can lower the blood sugar impact of carbohydrate foods.

As for what we politely call *regularity,* it's unlikely to be a problem. All that fat greases the skids. But you can take a sugar-free fiber supplement if you really feel the need.

Long Term Strategy

One trusts that you're not going to try to eat 1,000 calories per day, 90% from fat, forever. It is, as you may suspect, very restrictive. Furthermore, it's not enough protein for the long run.

However, Fat Fasting is a great strategy for losing five to ten pounds very quickly, and for jump-starting stalled weight loss. Dr. Atkins recommended that a Fat Fast last only three to five days. I've done it for eight days with no apparent ill effect. And as mentioned earlier, Dr. Benoit fat-fasted his subjects for ten days. I can't recommend taking it further than that.

Remember, we're not talking only about eating a very high-fat diet, we're also talking severe caloric restriction. It's the caloric restriction that is not appropriate for long-term use. After all, if you're eating only 1,000 calories per day, 900 of them from fat, that leaves only 100 calories for protein and carbs combined. Since protein runs four calories per gram, you can only get a maximum of 25 grams of protein per day on your Fat Fast, and that's if you eat no carbs at all, which is unlikely. Such a low protein intake is fine for the short run - as Benoit demonstrated, fat-fasting spares muscle mass - but it's insufficient for long-term use.

I asked **_Jacqueline Eberstein, RN_,** who was Dr. Atkins' right hand for thirty years, about his recommendation that people only Fat Fast very short term. She said that Dr. Atkins' concern was that people would abuse the Fat Fast, using it for quick weight loss, but never making the transition to a long-term low-carbohydrate diet. Using the Fat Fast sporadically, while eating a high-carb diet in between times, could lead, Atkins felt, to weight cycling, and eventually metabolic syndrome. Please, don't do this.

How to transition to a long-term strategy?

Here's my experience: For many years my low carb diet averaged around 1,800 to 2,200 calories per day, with somewhere around 100 to 120 grams of protein. Sadly, as I've aged, my body has gotten better at *gluconeogenesis* - converting protein to glucose. Though my blood sugar generally was normal, I started running pre-diabetic fasting blood sugar first thing in the morning. My doctor told me my liver was creating sugar from protein while I slept. He put me on metformin and Victoza, two blood-sugar-lowering medications. Even so, my morning sugar often ran in the 100 to 110 range.

Then I tried Fat Fasting. Very rapidly, my fasting blood sugar was running a tad too low - as low as 69 one morning. I dropped the Victoza - it was expensive and involved sticking myself with a needle.

After a week of Fat Fasting, I went to an every-other-day Fat Fast for several weeks, eating my usual low-carb fare on alternate days. My blood sugar got better and better, and I eventually dropped the metformin, too.

I have not continued with the every-other-day Fat Fast - I had a <u>cookbook to write</u> - but I have permanently reduced my protein intake to 70 to 80 grams per day, and increased my fat. Most days, I don't keep track of calories, but when I do, I find I'm getting more than 80% of my calories from fat. (Unless I drink alcohol, which skews the percentages.)

My blood sugar is not just normal, but considerably better than it was when I was on medication. When I had blood work done this past summer, my HbA1C (a measure of blood sugar over the previous three months) had dropped by 0.4 points as compared to last year - from 5.1 to 4.7 (that 5.1 indicated my blood sugar was normal overall, despite the high fasting sugar, but 4.7 is better).

Super-star blogger and podcaster, Jimmy Moore, has also reduced protein and increased fat, with the result that he has, at this writing, lost 60 pounds, and is crowing about his dramatic increase in energy.

If you've been low-carbing for a while and have plateaued at a higher weight than you'd hoped, or you still aren't getting the blood sugar levels you and your doctor want, you need to consider reducing protein intake permanently. Half a gram for every pound of body weight is about right (a gram per kilo if you live in the civilized world), with very little carbohydrate, and the rest of your calories coming from fat. These recipes will help.

Jackie Eberstein tells me that my every-other-day Fat Fast strategy was actually not a good idea, because it takes the body longer than that to really shift metabolism. Jackie is smarter, more educated, and far more experienced with the ins and outs of low carbohydrate nutrition than I. I will not try every-other-day Fat Fasting again, and cannot recommend it.

Instead, consider using the Fat Fast to break stalls, or if, despite a low-carbohydrate diet, your weight creeps up a few pounds. You might include a three to five day Fat Fast monthly or quarterly.

Jackie also says that in her current practice, <u>Controlled Carbohydrate Nutrition</u>, she often puts people on the Fat Fast five days per week, with an Atkins Induction Diet on the weekends. She says many people find this easier than Fat Fasting straight through.

Other Uses For These Recipes

These recipes are valuable for anyone who wants to be in nutritional ketosis.

Ketogenic diets have been used for decades to <u>control seizures in children</u>. I hope these recipes help epileptic children and their parents find more variety and interest in what can be a very restrictive diet.

Because cancer cells rely on glucose, there is growing interest in <u>ketogenic diets for cancer patients</u>.

Researchers Jeff Volek and Steve Phinney, in their groundbreaking book, <u>The Art and Science of Low Carbohydrate Performance</u>, have made a strong case for a ketogenic diet for athletes. Because it allows athletes to easily tap into stored fat for energy, instead of relying on limited stores of glycogen, a ketogenic diet has tremendous benefits, especially for endurance athletes.

Ketogenic diets also show promise for <u>preventing and treating Alzheimer's disease</u>. Since Alzheimer's has been tied to elevated blood sugar, and even dubbed type 3 diabetes, this is not surprising. Brains with Alzheimer's cannot properly use glucose for fuel, but can still run on ketones. Having watched helplessly as my mother disappeared into the twilight world of dementia, I find the reports that ketogenic diets are improving and even reversing Alzheimer's exciting beyond all telling.

I hope the recipes in this book will be useful for folks in all these groups.

What is Nutritional Ketosis and Why Is It Important?

by Jimmy Moore
(Updated from original article published on CarbSmart.com)

If you've been paying attention to the low-carb community lately, no doubt you have already heard about nutritional ketosis. Keen interest in this simple, yet important, idea has been one of the most exciting things to happen since I started blogging about this stuff in 2005. It just goes to show that despite the best efforts by the media and all the so-called health experts, hell-bent on discrediting healthy low-carb living, countless numbers of people who want to lose weight and attain optimal health still believe in its amazing benefits. There's certainly something there that warrants a closer look for those who have been struggling with their nutritional health goals.

If you've been following a low-carb lifestyle for any length of time, you probably already understand the importance of being in a ketogenic state, in which your body switches from using carbohydrates to using fat - both dietary and stored body fat - and ketone bodies as its primary fuel sources. The late, great Dr. Robert C. Atkins made this key concept the centerpiece of his best-selling books. Unfortunately, dietary ketosis has been severely maligned by Dr. Atkins' detractors as somehow being a dangerous state. Ketosis has a mistaken negative association with the truly dangerous and potentially fatal diabetic ketoacidosis that most frequently occurs in type 1 diabetics.

Another problem with using the term ketosis alone, as Dr. Atkins did throughout his work, is that it neglects to communicate any concrete, practical meaning regarding what it takes to get there. There are true benefits from ketosis, so this understanding is crucial. This is why I believe the phrase nutritional ketosis is a better way of framing the idea of becoming keto-adapted or fat-adapted through the use of a well-formulated high-fat, adequate- (moderate-) protein, low-carb diet. Until you get the macronutrient mix that is right for YOU, the health benefits of nutritional ketosis will continue to elude you.

The term nutritional ketosis has become popular in the low-carb community in recent years thanks to a series of books written by Drs. Stephen Phinney and Jeff Volek. They first used the term in their 2010 New York Times best-selling book, <u>The New Atkins For A New You</u> (written with Dr. Eric Westman). Phinney and Volek continued to use and define nutritional ketosis in their subsequent books, <u>The Art And Science of Low Carbohydrate Living</u> and <u>The Art and Science of Low Carbohydrate Performance</u>. This branding of the nutritional ketosis concept has been the best addition to the low-carb vernacular since many stopped calling low-carb a diet and started calling it a lifestyle.

So what's the difference between nutritional ketosis and the ketosis that has been a part of the Atkins diet for the past four decades? It's a subtle but very important distinction. First, though, let me express my incredible gratitude to Dr. Atkins for helping to change my life through his diet. Starting at 410 pounds in 2004, I lost 180 pounds that year and my life has never been the same. I'm honored and blessed to have a very popular health blog called Livin' La Vida Low-Carb, and three top-ranked iTunes podcasts (The Livin' La Vida Low-Carb Show, Ask The Low-Carb Experts, and Low-Carb Conversations), dedicated to spreading the message of low-carb living to the masses.

Though I never had the privilege of meeting him face to face, nothing I am doing today would have been possible without the inspiration and education that came from that amazing man. His legacy is still making ripples in the world nearly a decade after his tragic death following a slip-and-fall accident on an icy New York City sidewalk. His memory lives on through those of us who have picked up the baton and continued the race. God bless you, Dr. Atkins, for saving my life, and the lives of millions of others who benefit from your passionate zeal about low-carbohydrate nutrition, and what it can do for those who want to become healthy.

If Dr. Atkins were still around, I'm sure he'd be all in favor of this notion of nutritional ketosis. So what exactly is the distinction between nutritional ketosis and Atkins? Nutritional ketosis is ketosis, but ketosis may not necessarily be nutritional ketosis. Traditionally, ketosis has been measured with urine testing strips. These turn some shade of pink or purple when you are excreting ketones (acetoacetate) in your urine. But in their book The Art and Science of Low Carbohydrate Performance, Drs. Phinney and Volek recommend measuring blood ketones (beta-hydroxybutyrate) as a better and more reliable way of gauging ketone levels, allowing you to aim for the optimal range of 0.5 to 3.0 mm. The two most popular brands of blood ketone meters are Precision Xtra and Nova Max Plus. Both provide invaluable information about your level of nutritional ketosis. While test strips for these meters can be pricey, ranging from $1 to $6 per strip, it's worth knowing exactly where you stand when it comes to your low-carb lifestyle. A Google search will help you turn up the cheapest sources for a monitor and strips.

If you haven't yet tested your blood ketone levels and want to take a peek at how well you are doing on your chosen low-carb plan, I highly encourage you to pick up a meter and test for yourself. When I did this for the first time in May 2012, I was shocked to see my blood ketones measuring in at a paltry 0.3. I'd been eating what I thought was a pretty good high-fat, moderate-protein, low-carb diet for close to nine years! But upon closer examination, I realized that I was making some mistakes in my low-carb plan that prevented me from attaining nutritional ketosis. You need to avoid those mistakes if you want to experience the incredible health benefits that come from being in the sweet spot of low-carb living.

My Five Low-Carb Mistakes And How Nutritional Ketosis Rescued Me From Them

by Jimmy Moore (Updated from original article published on CarbSmart.com)

I've been doing my own personal n=1 experiment of nutritional ketosis since May 2012, reporting about it on my blog every 30 days. The longer I've been eating to produce enough blood ketones to turn myself into a fat-burning machine, the more I've learned about the mistakes I was making that were actually preventing me from reaching the level of nutritional ketosis needed to produce fat loss and improve various metabolic markers. Correcting these mistakes has helped me effortlessly shed a significant amount of weight, lower my blood sugar and A1c number, improve my lipid panel, and so much more. The following is not a comprehensive list of the common low-carb mistakes. However, these are worth a closer look if you are struggling with your weight and health goals. You just might be surprised!

1. Consuming too much protein.

What?! But I thought a low-carb diet was supposed to be high-protein! That is what we hear out there, don't we? The reality is that a well-formulated, low-carb diet is actually high in FAT, not protein. I bet you never thought that protein could hinder your weight loss - but it can. Why? Here's the word: **GLUCONEOGENESIS!** Say whoawhat? When you consume excess protein, your liver transforms it into glucose (sugar). If you are eating a lot of lean meats like chicken breasts, turkey, and lower-fat cuts of beef or pork, you might be defeating the purpose of your low-carb lifestyle. Try choosing fattier cuts of meat and controlling the absolute amount of protein you are eating (I aim for 12% of my total calorie intake) to see how that impacts your blood ketone levels.

2. Using urine ketone testing sticks to measure ketosis.

This is a biggie! Low-carbers have long relied on urine ketone test sticks (commonly sold as *Ketostix*) to detect the level of acetoacetate the body is excreting. Watching the sticks magically turn light pink to dark purple has always fascinated low-carb dieters, myself included, making us feel we are doing something constructive. It feels like a reward for our efforts. Unfortunately, these pee sticks are inexact. Further, they don't measure the specific kind of ketones your body can use as fuel. As I learned in *The Art and Science of Low Carbohydrate Performance*, it's better to test your blood for *beta*-hydroxybutyrate. This indicates whether or not you are keto-adapted, burning fat, and using ketones for fuel - the true essence of nutritional ketosis. You're looking for a level between 0.5 to 3.0 millimolar for optimal fat loss and keto-adapted performance. As I said earlier, you'll need a blood ketone meter, like the Precision Xtra from Abbott, to see where you stand. The information gained from measuring blood ketones instead of urine ketones is solid gold for knowing how well you are doing on your healthy low-carb eating plan!

3. Not eating enough dietary fat.

One of the lingering effects of the low-fat propaganda of the past three-plus decades is the idea that dietary fat is harmful, that it will clog your arteries and make you fat. So it's probably not surprising to hear that many who begin a low-carb diet simultaneously cut their fat intake with the best of intentions. They erroneously think that if low-carb is good, then low-fat *and* low-carb is dietary nirvana. But that's a fatal flaw in attempting to get into nutritional ketosis, stave off hunger and cravings, and experience the benefits that come from eating this way. Even if you think you're consuming enough high-fat foods, you may need to ramp it up a bit more. I'm eating around 85% of my calories from dietary fat during my n=1 experiment. I'll share some high-fat foods you can consume in a moment, but the key is to get creative and don't fear the fat. While you may not necessarily need to eat 85% of your calories in the form of fat, like I do, you'd be surprised how adding just a bit more fat to your diet can make all the difference in helping you to reach therapeutic levels of nutritional ketosis, shed pounds, and gain the health benefits that come with it.

4. Eating too often/too much food.

What's this? Is he talking about calories on a low-carb diet? Yes and no. Yes, it is indeed possible to eat beyond satiety and consume more food than you really need. But if there's anything I've learned about what happens to the body once you become keto-adapted, it's this: hunger is completely zapped, you *forget* to eat, and you generally feel energized and mentally alert while going many hours between meals. When you are producing sufficient ketone bodies - remember, that's between 0.5 to 3.0 millimolar - your body and brain are fueled efficiently.

I've fallen into a regular pattern of eating a calorie-sufficient set of meals with 85% fat, 12% protein, and 3% carbohydrate, consuming high-quality, nutrient-dense, real, whole foods. Consuming even one meal with this macronutrient makeup can keep me satiated for upwards of 12 to 24 hours. As you can imagine, this period of spontaneous intermittent fasting helps lower overall food and calorie consumption naturally without feeling miserably hungry between meals. Too many people habitually eat three full meals and two snacks daily because they always have and their fluctuating blood sugar levels required them to do so. But if you allow your cultural paradigms about food to shift from eating by the clock to eating when hunger kicks in, you might be pleasantly surprised to see your blood ketones increase and healthful weight loss commence.

5. Failing to stabilize blood sugar levels.

You might be wondering, *What does blood sugar have to do with nutritional ketosis?* Why should you worry about your blood glucose levels if you're not a diabetic? The reality is **EVERYONE** should be using a glucometer, easily accessible from any pharmacy or Walmart. That's the only way to know exactly what our blood sugar numbers are. Keeping carbohydrate intake to your personal level of tolerance, moderating your protein intake to match your metabolic needs, and eating ample amounts of satiating fats, will lower your fasting blood sugars into the 80s and even the 70s. When I first began my blood ketone experiment, my fasting blood sugar was regularly in the upper 90s to lower 100s. Once I attained an average blood ketone level of 2.0 millimolar over a period of time, my blood sugars suddenly dropped to an ideal level. Normalized blood sugar has kept my hunger at bay, regulated my mood, and given me a sense of well-being not experienced with the roller-coaster ride that alternating hyperglycemia and hypoglycemia produce. Get your blood sugar regulated and nutritional ketosis will be so much easier to attain. Conversely, nutritional ketosis will help you regulate your blood sugar. The two work hand-in-hand.

12 Healthy High-Fat Foods Perfect For Nutritional Ketosis

by Jimmy Moore (Updated from original article published on CarbSmart.com)

The most frequent question I've received from people about this by far has been, *What the heck are you eating?*

It's a fantastic question as I have consistently had blood ketone levels over 2.0 millimolar for most of this experiment. I have been reluctant to share my exact menus - they work for me, but some people may not need to eat exactly like I do to experience similar results; others may need to be even more strict. The best thing for you to do is test to see how you respond to various foods and adjust accordingly. We are all different and require varying levels of fat, protein, and carbohydrate for our specific metabolic needs. If you are like me and are metabolically deranged from years of poor nutritional choices prior to finding low-carb, it may be necessary to cut your carbohydrate intake down to the bare minimum, and reduce protein as well.

One of the major keys to my success with nutritional ketosis has been a very deliberate increase in fat consumption. I haven't been afraid to consume copious amounts of fat on my low-carb diet; in the absence of carbs, it is the body's fuel source. But pushing fat levels even higher while restricting carbohydrate and protein has made all the difference in the world. I remember when I first began this experiment, I got a lot of e-mails from readers who asked how I got my fat consumption up to 85% of my calories. Some joked, *What are you doing, drinking butter?* I can't help but laugh at this notion, but it does give me a teachable moment about the differences in the macronutrients.

When discussing the makeup of a very high-fat diet, it's important to remind people that one gram of dietary fat has nine calories, while carbohydrate and protein each have only four calories per gram. This means you need less than half the volume of fat to get the same calories you would receive from carbohydrate and protein. So it's really not as much fat as you would think. To help you figure out what to add into your diet to dramatically increase the amount of fat you are consuming, I've compiled a list of 12 high-fat foods that are perfect for your nutritional ketosis plan. If you eat these deliciously healthful, fatty (but not fattening) foods while reducing carbohydrate and protein, you can expect to experience the tremendous benefits that come from being in nutritional ketosis.

AVOCADOS

I remember the first time I tried an avocado
- people had told me about how incredible they
were. It was so hard I could barely get it open without slicing
my thumb off. I didn't know you have to let this fruit ripen until
the alligator skin gives way to light pressure. Once I had my first taste
of a fully-ripened Haas avocado, it was love at first bite! An avocado is cooling when
you're eating spicy foods, and offers a smooth texture change. I eat a whole avocado
almost everyday with my eggs and wouldn't imagine doing nutritional ketosis without it!

BUTTER

This one should be a *well, duh*, as butter is a staple of any good low-carb lifestyle. But
when you are attempting to achieve nutritional ketosis, it's even more important that you
deliberately add butter to foods, for both flavor and fat content. My favorite brand
of butter is grass-fed, unsalted, Kerrygold (in the silver wrapper).
Once you get a taste of this bright gold goodness you'll never
go back to anything else! I usually fry up two or three eggs in
two to three tablespoons of butter - it's an incredibly tasty way
to start the day. Why anyone would continue to eat
a man-made product like margarine thinking
it's a **healthy** food, when they could be eating
butter, is beyond my comprehension.

WHOLE EGGS

Speaking of eggs, they are one of the world's most perfect foods. If you care about
managing your weight and improving your health, you should be eating them. I buy eggs
from a local farmer who allows his chickens to forage in an open pasture, getting plenty
of sunshine. The payoff is the rich, dark orange color of the egg yolks - store-bought
eggs pale in comparison. If you can buy fresh eggs from a local farmer, do it. Even with
the premium price, they are still one of the most economical low-carb foods. Even when
money is tight, you can feed your family well. I eat eggs virtually every day because they
provide me with the perfect ratio of protein to fat to keep me on the straight and
narrow in my pursuit of nutritional ketosis. Please don't fall for
the idea that the yolk is somehow bad for you. Eating just
the egg whites is like driving a Mustang on the side streets
without ever getting on the interstate. You'll never
experience the full benefits of eating eggs until you
eat the whole egg!

COCONUT OIL

Other than grass-fed butter, my absolute favorite source of healthful, dietary saturated fat is coconut oil. Contrary to popular belief, adding this quality fat to your diet does not make everything you consume taste like coconuts. My favorite brand is **_Nutiva Certified Organic Extra Virgin Coconut Oil_**; it imparts a pleasantly sweet aroma with a very mild coconut flavor. I especially enjoy cooking my eggs in coconut oil along with sea salt and parsley; it gives them a nice *buttery* flavor. Because it is highly saturated, coconut oil has long been vilified as a nutritional demon. That misguided opinion is finally beginning to turn around. If you are trying to increase your level of blood ketones, then there's probably no better way to start than by adding coconut oil to your daily menus.

BACON

I don't have to convince anyone reading this to start eating more bacon, do I? Back in August, at the 2012 Ancestral Health Symposium, Harvard organic chemist Mat Lalonde extolled the virtues of consuming bacon. He noted that the fatty acid profile of this much-vilified food is actually pretty darn close to ideal. Of course, if you can get bacon from pastured pigs, that's even better! My wife Christine loves bacon and eats it almost every day. Healthy fats, perfect amount of protein, and minimal carbohydrates - what more could someone eating a low-carb diet ask? Bacon goes great with...well, everything. So eat up!

SOUR CREAM

If you are able to tolerate dairy, I can't imagine why you wouldn't want to add sour cream to just about everything you eat. It's such a rich source of fat while providing amazing flavor and luxurious texture to any food. I put sour cream on top of steak, eggs, even vegetables. Just a couple of tablespoons of sour cream will give your fat intake the boost it needs to help you get into that glorious state of nutritional ketosis. I use the full-fat versions of either Breakstone's or Daisy, depending on which is on sale, on something just about every day. Enjoy!

70% GROUND BEEF

What low-carb dieter doesn't like a nice hamburger? The key is to find the fattiest ground beef you can. This can be a challenge in this fat-phobic society. Most of the meats you'll find in your local grocery store are 85 to 90% lean, meaning they've cut most of the best part out of it! Look for 70% ground beef, and choose locally-farmed grass-fed beef whenever possible. EatWild.com can help you find a local source of grass-fed beef. The great thing about a burger is you can cook it in butter, add some cheese (see below), and spread some sour cream on it for a mouth-watering, low-carb, high-fat meal that will put you well on your way to reaching nutritional ketosis. WOO HOO!

FULL-FAT CHEDDAR CHEESE

Cheese is one of my favorite foods. Sadly, most people think Velveeta and American cheese are cheese. Nope! Not even close. They are highly-processed, cheese-like products that you really don't want to eat, no matter how low the carb counts might be. Hard cheeses like Cheddar, Monterey Jack, and Swiss are better choices. Find the ones you enjoy, and be sure to buy the full-fat versions. Selecting low-fat cheese defeats the purpose, and won't help you reach nutritional ketosis. Cheese is so versatile! Put it on just about anything, or eat it all by itself. I've found that spreading cream cheese (see below) between two slices of cheddar cheese is an excellent high-fat, moderate protein, low-carb snack. I've also found cheese adds the perfect extra ration of protein on days that I lift weights at the gym. Can you tell I love my cheese?

COCONUT

Growing up, I couldn't stand coconut. It wasn't the delightful, tropical flavor that bothered me, but the waxy, gritty texture. But the first time I ate the meat of a fresh coconut - on Grand Cayman Island during the annual Low-Carb Cruise - oh my gosh! I thought I'd died and gone to heaven. The best part about coconut is that its fatty goodness really jacks up those blood ketone levels. Mix some coconut into a smoothie in the morning and it will keep your hunger satisfied for hours on end. It's time to get cuckoo for coconuts!

DARK CHOCOLATE

You might be thinking to yourself, Say what? Dark chocolate? Are you kidding me? Nope, I'm not kidding. Lean in really close, because I've got a secret to share with you: I eat dark chocolate EVERY SINGLE DAY on my nutritional ketosis plan. Yep, I sure do! Sometimes I'll even have it with some of that grass-fed, unsalted, Kerrygold butter I mentioned - truly incredible. I'm not talking about cheap, fake dark chocolate or even the sugar-free ones you can buy in most stores. I have fallen head over heels for a brand of chocolate that is far superior to anything I've ever put in my mouth before –Taza 80% Stone Ground Dark Chocolate. This stuff contains little chunks of real cacao and even has real sugar in it (GASP!). But I eat a half and sometimes a whole bar of this daily with no negative impact on my blood sugar or blood ketone levels. It's got to be the cocoa butter that makes it such a perfect addition to my nutritional ketosis plan.

CREAM CHEESE

I said earlier that sour cream was amazing with virtually any food you could consume. Well, the same could be said about cream cheese! This stuff has an amazing fat profile that will give your meals the boost they need to help you reach nutritional ketosis. If you've never put cream cheese in your eggs before, let me tell you that's an experience you won't soon forget. It totally changes the texture of eggs; you may never eat them any other way again. I know of no better brand than Philadelphia cream cheese. Again - it bears repeating - beware of the lower-fat version. Read the label to make sure fat is the predominant ingredient and you'll be good to go.

LIQUID FISH OIL

Finally, I couldn't talk about healthful fats without telling you about fish oil. While you won't be adding this to your food, it is an important supplement to your diet, and will increase your blood ketones dramatically. I take two tablespoons of Carlson's lemon-flavored liquid cod liver oil (the Vitamin Shoppe brand of this is nearly identical and cheaper) daily to infuse my body with healthy omega-3 fats as part of my heart-healthy regimen. There are fish-oil capsules and tablets available at drug stores, but many of these may be rancid, and therefore counterproductive. That's why I prefer the liquid fish oil. In case you're worried about the fishy taste of this stuff, it's actually a delightfully pleasant lemony taste. I couldn't imagine going through my day without taking my liquid fish oil, and the resulting blood ketone levels make it worth it!

Be hyper-aware of the nutritional content of everything you put in your mouth. In our fat-phobic society, many of the foods listed above have lower-fat and lean versions. You don't want to consume those. Your lower-protein, low-carb nutritional ketosis plan requires high-fat levels to be optimally healthful.

So, are you ready to try nutritional ketosis for yourself? Then you are definitely in for a treat with this amazing new cookbook designed to put you on track to incredible success in your low-carb lifestyle. Don't get discouraged or dismayed if you don't see the kind of results you think you should. Just keep tweaking, testing, and turning to the things I've shared with you and be patient, persistent, and passionate about doing this like nothing you've done before. In the end, this is all about YOU and producing the changes in your weight and health that you so desperately desire and deserve. Believe me, I understand that, and hope you are able to experience all the benefits of nutritional ketosis by applying what you learn in this book. Remember: NEVER GIVE UP and YOU CAN DO THIS!

Fat Fast Ingredients

by Dana Carpender

All of the Fat Fast ingredients listed in this section can be found at Amazon.com by visiting our Fat Fast Ingredients for Fat Fast Cookbook page.

Coconut Oil

Because it is rich in saturated fats called medium-chain triglycerides, coconut oil is particularly ketogenic, making it especially suitable for Fat Fasting. It also stimulates thermogenesis - in other words, it increases body temperature slightly, burning off extra calories. Too, medium chain triglycerides can be used directly by the muscles for fuel, making them a source of quick energy. All of this makes coconut oil valuable to us.

Because it's highly saturated, coconut oil was mistakenly considered unhealthful for a long time, and was hard to find. (When I started buying it, only my local health food store had it - and they stocked it with the cosmetics, not the other cooking oils.) It is becoming more readily available; I can buy it at my local Kroger.

There are a few options with coconut oil:

Extra Virgin Coconut Oil: This is the gold standard; and likely the best for you. However, it is also very pricey, and has a distinct coconut aroma, which may or may not go well with a particular recipe.

Coconut Oil: Just plain coconut oil is more refined than extra virgin, but it's still loaded with the medium-chain triglycerides that fuel ketone production. It also is very bland, making it suitable for recipes where you feel a coconut note would be out of place. Considerably cheaper than extra-virgin, too.

Liquid Coconut Oil: In its native form, coconut oil is solid at room temperature, unless your house is pretty warm. This makes coconut oil unsuitable for making mayonnaise or salad dressing, or for adding to smoothies or other cold drinks. New to the market is liquid coconut oil - coconut oil that is liquid at room temperature. It is pricey. (I paid $28 for 20 fluid ounces!) However, if you are determined to stay in a strongly ketogenic state, it may be worth the investment. So far as I can tell, liquid coconut oil - mine is bottled by Nature's Way, a well-known herbal supplement company - is substantially similar to medium-chain-triglyceride oil, long sold as an athletic supplement. Liquid coconut oil has a coconut aroma, which may or may not suit a particular recipe.

Coconut Butter

Let me be clear: COCONUT BUTTER IS NOT THE SAME AS COCONUT OIL. I emphasize this because I have had so many questions about it, and more than a few readers have had recipes fail because they used coconut oil where a recipe called for coconut butter.

Coconut butter (Nutiva calls it Coconut Manna) is to coconut what peanut butter is to peanuts, or almond butter is to almonds: Simply coconut meat ground to a paste. As word about the healthful properties of coconut spreads, coconut butter is gaining popularity. I have used it in several recipes in this book.

You can buy coconut butter at health food stores or, like everything else in the world, online. However, at this writing, jarred coconut butter is running $12 to $16 per pound. This is why you'll find a recipe for coconut butter in this book - it's a snap to make if you have a decent food processor, and unsweetened, shredded coconut in bulk is quite cheap.

Coconut Milk

There are now two kinds of coconut milk on the market: The thick, traditional stuff that comes in cans, and a thinner, more pourable variety that comes in cartons like dairy milk, soy milk, and almond milk. These recipes use the thick, rich, canned stuff. Look for it in the international foods aisle at your grocery store, with the Asian foods. Buy the full-fat variety, not the low-fat, of course.

Shirataki Noodles

The only genuinely low-carb and low-calorie noodle I know of, shirataki are traditional Japanese noodles made from the root of the konyaku or konjac plant. They are sometimes labeled yam noodles or yam bean noodles, but that's a mistranslation; konjac is not related to sweet potatoes. (Technically, yams aren't related to sweet potatoes, either, but that's another story. The two terms are used interchangeably in the USA.) Konjac is the source of a fiber called glucomannan, and that's what shirataki noodles are made of.

They come in two varieties: Traditional and tofu shirataki. The traditional shirataki are translucent and sort of gelatinous - for lack of a better description, they're very Asian. I like them, but only in Asian recipes - you'll find a recipe in this book for sesame noodles, for instance. My friend and fellow cookbook author Judy Barnes Baker (Nourished: A Cookbook for Health, Weight Loss, and Metabolic Balance) tells me that Nasoya now makes a noodle called Pasta Zero that has the flavor and texture of tofu shirataki without the soy. 1 gram of usable carb per serving. At this writing I have not tried Pasta Zero, but you can bet I'm going to! If you can't find them locally, you may well be able to special-order them through your local health food store.

Tofu shirataki, as the name strongly suggests, have a little tofu added to the glucomannan fiber. This makes them white, and gives them texture that is more tender than the gelatinous, traditional variety. They're certainly not identical to the Italian pasta we're all familiar with, but they're considerably closer than the traditional variety, while still being super-low-carb and super-low-calorie. Unlike traditional shirataki, I like the tofu variety in all sorts of recipes - mac and cheese, chicken noodle soup, Fettuccini Alfredo, you name it.

The great thing about shirataki is that because they are so low in carbs and calories, all you have to do is add some sort of high-fat topping to them and you not only have a Fat Fast meal, you have a full-sized serving. With most Fat Fast portion sizes being so small, shirataki noodles are a real ace in the hole. When you get tired of nibbling a quarter-cup of macadamia nuts, you can sit down to a full, satisfying bowl of food.

Shirataki come pre-hydrated in a pouch full of liquid, so they don't require the ten minutes or so of boiling that standard pasta needs. However, I find them best with a little quick-and-simple prep:

Put a strainer in the sink. Snip open your shirataki pouch, and dump them into the strainer. You will notice that the liquid they've been packaged in smells unappealingly fishy. Panic not.

Dump your drained shirataki into a microwaveable bowl, and nuke them on high for two minutes. Back into the strainer and drain them again - I bounce the strainer up and down a little, to knock off even more liquid. Nuke for another minute, and drain one more time.

Why all this heating and draining? Because without it, shirataki will exude liquid into your sauce, making for a watery finished product. You're getting the excess liquid out of them. I find this also does away with the fish smell and improves the texture.

Shirataki noodles are really long - apparently long noodles are considered good luck in Japan. I use my kitchen shears to snip across them in an X pattern, so I have more manageable lengths.

Shirataki will disintegrate if you freeze them. Keep this in mind if ordering in the winter.

Like other pastas, shirataki come in different shapes. I have mostly used House brand tofu shirataki, which come in spaghetti, angel hair, fettuccini, and macaroni shapes. I like the fettuccini and macaroni shapes best. I find that traditional shirataki is most often available in spaghetti-like strands, but have also seen it in little rice-shaped bits, similar to orzo.

One more thing: For those of you avoiding soy, tofu shirataki have only a teeny bit of soy in them. I did the math, and it's like a teaspoon of tofu per serving. Since they're about the only source of soy in my diet, I don't worry about it, but make your own decisions.

Liquid Stevia Extract

Stevia is a calorie-free and carb-free sweetener derived from the leaves of a South American shrub. This sounds ideal, but for a long time I didn't use much stevia. It was too sweet, it had a bitter aftertaste, and I found it difficult to use.

However, I have discovered liquid stevia extracts, and I find them far easier to use than the powdered stevia extracts. Liquid stevia extracts come in little dropper bottles; there are both alcohol-based and alcohol-free versions. I don't find a lot of difference between them in use. Liquid stevia comes plain, i.e., just sweet, and in flavors. I have used both chocolate and French vanilla liquid stevia extract in some of these recipes.

Note: Most liquid stevia extracts take roughly 6-8 drops to get the equivalent of 1 teaspoon sugar in sweetness. That means that you can substitute, say, 2 teaspoons of granular Splenda for 15 drops of liquid stevia extract. Other sweeteners should give their sweetness equivalency on the labels; if they don't, try their websites. Keep in mind, though, that if a recipe calls for a flavored stevia extract, you'll lose that extra flavor; you may want to add vanilla or chocolate extract to make up for it. Do not assume that the sugar-free coffee flavoring syrups are interchangeable with the liquid stevia extracts - they are far less concentrated.

Also, please take it to read that all sweetener quantities include the words "or to taste." I mean, who's in charge here, you or the food?

Erythritol

This is only mentioned in one recipe, but it's a really good recipe. Erythritol is a sugar alcohol or polyol sweetener that is almost completely unabsorbed by the body, and therefore can be counted as zero carbs. Also, unlike some of the sugar alcohols, erythritol has very little gastric impact. It's become one of my go-to ingredients. Look for it at health food stores or order online.

Liquid Sucralose

Because sucralose, bulked with maltodextrin, is used to make Splenda measure cup-for-cup like sugar, Splenda is not carb-free, no matter what the label says. (I count it at 0.5 grams of carb per teaspoon, if I'm being really careful.) Liquid sucralose, however, is carb-free, and has therefore become very popular in the low-carb community. I like the EZ Sweetz brand.

Sugar-Free Coffee Flavoring Syrups

These are the sort of syrups you find at coffee places. I know of three brands of sugar-free coffee flavoring syrups: DaVinci Gourmet, Torani, and Monin O'Free. I have tried them all, and found them all to be terrific, versatile ingredients. I keep vanilla, chocolate, caramel, and hazelnut sugar-free syrups on hand, and have tried many others. If you're a coffee drinker, you may enjoy a breakfast feeding of a cup of coffee with ¼ cup heavy cream plus whatever syrup appeals to you that day.

A General Word About Sweeteners

One of the great tribulations of my professional life is the Sweetener Wars. No matter what sweetener I use in a recipe, someone will complain. Some feel artificial sweeteners are terribly dangerous, while others find stevia difficult to use or too expensive. Others demand to know why I'm not using xylitol (It's toxic to dogs, and I have three), or why I use any sweeteners at all. Truly, I don't care; my feelings will not be hurt if you substitute the sweetener of your choice in any of these recipes. Suit yourself. And if you prefer to use no sweeteners at all, there are plenty of non-sweet recipes in the book for you to enjoy.

Guar, Xanthan, and Glucomannan Thickeners

These three odd sounding items, Guar Gum, Xanthan Gum, and Glucomannan Powder are thickeners made from finely milled soluble fibers. They add a velvety texture to soups, smoothies and sauces. Since these thickeners consist only of fiber, they can be discounted on a Fat Fast.

I consider these three pretty much interchangeable, and can get them all at my local health food stores. Keep an old salt shaker filled with one of these thickeners by the stove. When you want to thicken something, start whisking first, then sprinkle the thickener lightly over the surface. If you just dump in some thickener and then whisk, you'll get lumps. Use a light hand with these thickeners, and stop when your dish is not quite as thick as you want - they continue to thicken on standing.

Salt

I would like to put in a word here in favor of salt. Not only does it make things taste better, but it is also an essential nutrient. Yes, an essential nutrient; a severe deficiency can and will kill. Hyponatremia - low blood sodium - is fairly common among low-carbohydrate dieters (this, from Drs. Phinney and Volek), because once chronically high insulin levels are lowered, the kidneys starts eliminating sodium properly; at the same time the low-carb dieter, having ditched most processed foods, will be getting considerably less dietary sodium.

Low sodium levels can make you feel weak, achy, dizzy (especially when you stand up) and headache-y. Not fun, as I happen to know.

So don't deliberately avoid salt on your Fat Fast, or any low-carb diet, and if you have any of the above symptoms, add more.

I very much recommend spending the money for <u>mined sea salt</u> from ancient sea beds. It's a terrific source of trace minerals, and because it was deposited eons ago, it's not polluted. It also tastes better than grocery store salt. I buy <u>Real Salt</u> brand at my health food store, and also have some pink Himalayan sea salt in the house.

Vege-Sal

<u>Vege-Sal</u> is a seasoned salt, but don't think Lawry's Seasoned Salt - it's much more subtle. It's largely salt with powdered, dried vegetables. It's not essential in any of these recipes, but I think it improves all sorts of things. Vege-Sal is available at health food stores and online.

Ghee

<u>Ghee</u> is the Indian name for clarified butter - butter with the milk solids removed. Some dairy-intolerant folks find that while they can't use regular butter, they have no problem with ghee. My local health food stores carry ghee in jars, and you may be able to find it in particularly comprehensive grocery stores; look for it with the Indian foods. I haven't called for ghee in any of these recipes, but if you can't eat butter due to lactose intolerance or other reasons, you could try using ghee in these recipes instead.

A Few Basic Recipes

First, we have a few recipes that you'll need in order to make some of the other recipes in this cookbook.

Ketonnaise

This recipe calls for liquid coconut oil, an ingredient that has only recently become available, and it is, uh... pricey. You could also use medium-chain-triglyceride (MCT) oil; it's marketed to athletes. Or just go with all olive oil. Don't use regular coconut oil, or you'll get mayo that's hard at room temperature, unless your room is pretty warm.

Ingredients

2 egg yolks

1 tablespoon wine vinegar

1 tablespoon lemon juice

1 teaspoon dry mustard

¼ teaspoon salt

1 dash Tabasco sauce

½ cup olive oil

½ cup liquid coconut oil or another ½ cup olive oil.

Instructions

1. Put everything but the oil in a clean, old jar with a lid – I use a salsa jar.

2. In a glass measuring cup with a pouring lip, combine the two oils. Have this standing by.

3. Immerse your stick blender in the egg-yolk mixture, and blend for several seconds, until it's uniform.

4. Now, keeping the blender running the whole time, very slowly pour in the oil – your stream should be about the diameter of a pencil lead. Work your blender up and down in the jar to make sure you mix the oil in thoroughly.

5. When your mayo is stiff, and the oil starts to puddle on top, you're done. Mine took all the oil, but you may have a little oil leftover in the cup. Just use it to fry something later on.

6. Cap and store in the fridge, of course.

Nutritional Information

16 servings of about 1 tablespoon, each with:
127 Calories;
14g Fat
(98.2% calories from fat);
trace Protein;
trace Carbohydrate;
trace Dietary Fiber;
0g Usable Carbs

Notes

I am unafraid of raw eggs; the rate of contamination of uncracked, properly refrigerated eggs is very low. If you're worried, look for pasteurized eggs.

Also, you can make this in your regular blender, if you like. You'll just need to transfer it to a jar, and wash the blender.

Coconut Butter

Coconut butter runs between $12 and $16 per pound at health food stores. But I can get shredded coconut for $3 per pound! This does require a pretty good food processor; my Cuisinart works great.

Ingredients

4   cups unsweetened, shredded coconut meat

Instructions

1. Super-simple: Dump the coconut in your food processor with the S-blade in place, and turn it on.

2. Set your oven timer for 10 minutes, and go do something else.

3. Come back, scrape down the sides of the food processor bowl with a rubber scraper, and run for another five to seven minutes or so—it should flow in the bottom of the bowl.

4. Scrape into a jar or snap-top container. Doesn't even really need refrigeration, unless you're planning to keep it for months and months.

Nutritional Information

4 cups of finely-shredded, unsweetened coconut yields about 1 cup of butter. Figure 8 servings of 2 tablespoons, each with: 142 Calories; 13g Fat (80.2% calories from fat); 1g Protein; 6g Carbohydrate; 4g Dietary Fiber; 2g Usable Carbs

Notes

If you can only get unsweetened coconut in large flakes, they'll work fine, too; I just don't have a measurement of how many cups of flakes for a cup of butter.

Here in Bloomington, Indiana, we have two health food grocers. One only carries shredded coconut in little seven-ounce packages, for something like $5. The other has it in a bin in the bulk foods section for a big $3 per pound. It's worth looking for the bulk coconut! Too, try to find a store with a fairly brisk turnover. The fresher your coconut, the better your coconut butter will be.

Coconut Sour Cream

Some of you are avoiding dairy. Fortunately, it is possible to make quite nice sour coconut cream — I learned how to do this while writing 500 Paleo Recipes. Here's how:

Ingredients	1 can coconut milk	1 teaspoon yogurt starter

Instructions

1. Let a can of coconut milk sit in the fridge overnight, without disturbing it. Then open it, taking off the whole lid. You will find that the fatty part of the coconut milk - the coconut cream - has risen to the top. Scoop this off into a snap-top container. You can discard the watery part, or give it to the dog, water a plant, whatever.

2. Let the coconut cream soften at room temperature. Now whisk in a teaspoon of yogurt starter - or, for that matter, of yogurt; you can buy coconut yogurt at health food stores if you have to be really, strictly dairy-free. I have also pulled apart a probiotic capsule and used the contents as a starter, with good results. Just get some nice acidophilus and/or bifidus bacteria in there. Whisk the whole thing up thoroughly.

3. Put on the lid, and put your coconut cream in a warm place. A yogurt maker is ideal, if you have one. I line a mixing bowl with an old heating pad set on low, and settle the container down in it, then drape a tea towel across the top to hold in the heat. You could also put your container over a floor heat register, with a mixing bowl inverted over it to hold in the heat. Anyway, let your coconut cream incubate for 12 hours or so - I let mine sit overnight.

Nutritional Information

Unfortunately, I don't have nutrition stats on this; I don't know how to calculate for the watery part that's discarded. I would count it the same as dairy sour cream, and call it near enough for government work.

The good news is that the fat in coconut cream is more ketogenic than the fat in dairy sour cream.

Notes

You may find your cultured coconut cream looks kind of gray and uninspiring when it's done incubating. Refrigerate it for a day, and you will find it becomes much more appetizing. I used this coconut sour cream in many recipes while writing 500 Paleo Recipes, and it worked just like dairy sour cream, though of course it has a coconut flavor. It's also slightly sweeter than dairy sour cream. Still, you can substitute it one-for-one in any recipe in this book that calls for sour cream.

Recipes Under 80% Fat

We have here a few recipes that come in at just under the 80% fat mark, but were too good to leave out. Be sure to balance them with something from the 90% fat or above range.

Fat Fast Asian Noodles

Super-satisfying! This is like sesame noodles, and you can make it right in the bowl.

Ingredients

1 packet traditional Shirataki noodles or tofu shirataki noodles

1 tablespoon coconut oil

1 tablespoon natural peanut butter

1 tablespoon chicken broth

½ teaspoon dark sesame oil

½ teaspoon grated ginger root

1 drop liquid sucralose or liquid stevia extract

1 clove garlic

1 teaspoon soy sauce

1 scallion

Instructions

1. Dump the shirataki into a strainer in the sink, rinse, and drain well.

2. Put in a microwaveable bowl, and nuke for two minutes.

3. Drain again, and nuke for another minute or two.

4. Drain one more time.

5. Snip across the noodles a few times with your kitchen shears.

6. Now measure everything except the scallion into the bowl.

7. Stir till it all blends into a sauce.

8. Slice the scallion on top, and eat.

Nutritional Information

Per Serving: 285 Calories;
24g Fat
(74.9% calories from fat);
6g Protein;
12g Carbohydrate;
5g Dietary Fiber;
7g Usable Carbs

Lime Cheesecake Minis

Amy says: Cheesecake as a Fat Fast meal? Yes please. When I made these for my family, they didn't last long. You might want to make a double batch if you don't live alone.

Ingredients

8   ounces cream cheese, softened

½   cup heavy whipping cream

1   tablespoon vanilla

3   whole eggs

6   packets True Lime

Sugar-free sweetener to equal 12 teaspoons of sugar

Instructions

1. Using an electric mixer, beat cream cheese and heavy cream until smooth. Add remaining ingredients and mix well.

2. Pour batter into greased ramekins and place on a cookie sheet. Bake at 350 degrees F for 30 to 40 minutes, until knife inserted in center comes out clean.

3. Set on a rack until cool enough to handle, then refrigerate until ready to serve.

Nutritional Information

6 servings, each with:
255 Calories;
23g Fat
(79.7% calories from fat);
6g Protein;
7g Carbohydrate;
0g Dietary Fiber;
7g Usable Carbs

Lime Cheesecake Minis

Broccoli Cheese Soup

Amy says: This is an adaptation of a recipe I put together several years ago, modeled after the high-carb version of my aunt's cheese soup. It's warm, filling, and tasty. It's perfect for those times when you're hankering for comfort food.

Ingredients

- 2 cups broccoli florets, steamed
- 4 ounces cream cheese, softened
- 2 cups water
- ¼ cup heavy whipping cream
- ½ cup chicken broth
- 1 teaspoon salt
- 1 cup Cheddar cheese

  Pepper, to taste

Instructions

1. Steam the broccoli florets till tender. Mix ½ cup of the broccoli, all the cream cheese, ½ cup of the water, and all the heavy cream in a blender until smooth.

2. Pour this mixture into a pot or large saucepan. Add chicken broth, rest of broccoli, and rest of water and mix. Over medium heat, bring to a simmer.

3. Once heated, add your Cheddar cheese and mix until melted and completely blended. Add pepper to taste.

Nutritional Information
4 servings, each with:
280 Calories;
25g Fat
(79.3% calories from fat);
11g Protein;
4g Carbohydrate;
1g Dietary Fiber;
3g Usable Carbs

Broccoli Cheese Soup

Fat Fast Scramble

Amy says: While this would obviously be great for breakfast, it's just as delicious any other time of the day. It's another quick and easy meal that has become a favorite of mine, especially on busy days when I'm short on time.

Ingredients

1 egg

2 teaspoons butter, melted

2 teaspoons heavy cream

Salt and pepper to taste

1 tablespoon ham cubes, diced small

¼ cup Cheddar cheese

Instructions

1. Beat together egg, butter, cream, salt and pepper.

2. Spray a small skillet with olive oil, if needed, and heat over burner set on medium.

3. Pour egg mixture into pan. With a spatula or turner, mix until eggs start to set.

4. Add ham and cheese, mixing until cheese is melted and eggs are set.

Nutritional Information

1 serving, with:
240 Calories;
21g Fat
(79.9% calories from fat);
11g Protein;
1g Carbohydrate;
0g Dietary Fiber;
1g Usable Carbs

Fat Fast Scramble

Recipes 80% to 83% Fat

In the general run of things, these are certainly high fat recipes. But for Fat-Fasting, they're at the bottom of the range. So enjoy these recipes, but be sure to balance them from something higher fat at another "feeding."

Hot "Cereal"

Want a comforting winter breakfast? Here it is. Add a sprinkle of cinnamon if you like.

Ingredients

- 1 ½ tablespoons ground pecans (I find this labeled pecan meal or pecan powder)
- 1 ½ tablespoons shredded coconut meat
- 1 tablespoon flax seed meal
- 1 pinch salt
- ½ cup boiling water, or to taste
- 2 tablespoons heavy cream
- Splenda or sweetener of choice, to taste

Nutritional Information

Per Serving: 247 Calories;
24g Fat
(80.7% calories from fat);
5g Protein;
8g Carbohydrate;
6g Dietary Fiber;
2g Usable Carbs

Instructions

1. Measure the pecans, coconut, and flax seed meal into a bowl, and add the salt. Stir them all together.

2. Add the boiling water, and stir it all up. Let it sit for just a minute or two.

3. Add the cream and sweetener of choice, and eat!

Hot "Cereal"

Cocoa-Coconut Candy

Easy, but oh-so-good! I make these even when I'm not fat fasting, to get a kick of energy-spiking medium chain triglycerides before working out.

Ingredients

1 cup coconut butter

1 ounce unsweetened baking chocolate, melted

2 tablespoons coconut oil, melted

30 drops liquid stevia extract - chocolate or French vanilla flavor, your choice

Instructions

1. Combine everything in your food processor, and run until it's well-combined - you'll need to scrape down the sides once or twice.

2. Spoon by level tablespoonfuls onto waxed paper, and refrigerate. You should get 16 candies; 2 to a serving.

Nutritional Information	2g Protein;
8 servings,	7g Carbohydrate;
each with: 189 Calories;	4g Dietary Fiber;
19g Fat	3g Usable Carbs
82.8% calories from fat;	

Cocoa-Coconut Candy

Chocolate Almond Instant "Pudding"

Rebecca says: When doing a fat fast, I like to throw in a little decadence. I saw a recipe on the Internet for a dish called keto pudding that included mascarpone cheese. After paying over $5 for a small amount of that cheese, I changed the recipe to exclude it, added almond extract, and it tastes just as good and very rich.

Ingredients

- ½ cup organic sour cream
- 2 teaspoons unsweetened cocoa powder
- 8 drops liquid stevia extract, flavored or unflavored
- 10 drops pure almond extract (or to taste)

Instructions

1. Put all the ingredients into a small bowl and stir until well mixed.
2. Get a spoon and enjoy!

Nutritional Information	
1 serving with 255 Calories;	6.4g Carbohydrate;
23.4g Fat	1g Fiber;
82.6% calories from fat;	5.4g Usable Carbs
4.7g Protein;	

Bacon Cheddar Deviled Eggs

Amy says, These deviled eggs pretty much utilize all my favorite ingredients. My daughter's first response after trying one was, Wow, these are filling! And you can easily fit two into your Fat Fast feeding.

Ingredients

6 eggs

½ ripe avocado

4 tablespoons mayonnaise

2 tablespoons Cheddar cheese

3 slices bacon, fried and crumbled (or use 2 tablespoons real bacon bits)

Salt and pepper, to taste

Instructions

1. Hard boil eggs. While eggs are boiling, cut an avocado in half and remove seed. Scoop out the inside of one half and mash with a fork (half a medium-sized avocado will yield about ¼ cup). Set aside.

2. Once the eggs have cooled, peel them and cut in half lengthwise. Scoop out the yolks and put them into a small mixing bowl.

3. Mash egg yolks with a fork until fine and crumbly, then add mayo, mashed avocado, cheese, bacon, salt, and pepper. Stir until well mixed.

4. With a spoon, scoop out small mounds of the yolk mixture and fill the egg cavities. Store in the fridge until ready to serve.

Nutritional Information
6 servings (2 pieces),
each with: 168 Calories;
16g Fat
(80.8% calories from fat);
8g Protein;
2g Carbohydrate;
trace Dietary Fiber;
2g Usable Carbs

Boursin Stuffed Mushrooms

These are the easiest stuffed mushrooms I ever made, and some of the best. Make a whole batch, stash in the fridge, and warm in the microwave as needed.

Ingredients

1 pound mushrooms

8 ounces Boursin cheese (about a package and a half)

½ cup chicken broth

Paprika to garnish

Instructions

1. Preheat the oven to 350 degrees F. Remove the stems from the mushrooms, reserving them for another use.

2. Fill each mushroom with Boursin, arranging them in a baking pan as you go.

3. Pour just enough chicken broth around the mushrooms to film the bottom of the pan. Sprinkle lightly with paprika.

4. Bake for 30 to 40 minutes. Serve hot.

Nutritional Information

5 Servings, each with:
207 Calories;
20g Fat
(80.7% calories from fat);
5g Protein;
6g Carbohydrate;
1g Dietary Fiber;
5g Usable Carbs

Boursin Stuffed Mushrooms

Simple Avocado Salad

I just love this. One of my favorite ways to eat avocados.

Ingredients

½ avocado

2 teaspoons olive oil

¼ lime

Salt and pepper

Instructions

1. Just slice your avocado half (If you don't have an avocado slicer, it's a gadget worthy of drawer-space) and arrange the slices on a plate.

2. Sprinkle with the olive oil, squeeze the lime over it, and salt and pepper to taste. That's it. Yummy!

Nutritional Information		
One Serving: 246 Calories;	(83.0% calories from fat);	3g Dietary Fiber;
24g Fat	2g Protein;	6g Usable Carbs
	9g Carbohydrate;	

Guacamole

Of course you're not eating tortilla chips, but you could scoop this with celery or pepper strips, or just eat it with a spoon!

Ingredients

1 tablespoon minced red onion

½ garlic clove, crushed

1 avocado - a little black one, good and ripe

¼ lime

1 tablespoon olive oil

2 dashes hot sauce, or to taste

Salt to taste

½ tablespoon minced cilantro, optional

Instructions

1. Have your onion minced and your garlic crushed and in a bowl before you start.

2. Halve your avocado and use a spoon to scoop the flesh out into the bowl.

3. Use a fork to mash up the avocado. Don't go for a super-smooth texture, leave some little lumps of avocado.

4. Now squeeze in the lime juice, add the olive oil, hot sauce, salt, and cilantro, if using. Stir it up and serve immediately! Guacamole just doesn't hold very well.

Note: If you're not Fat Fasting, just staying in nutritional ketosis, try this guacamole spread on a rib eye steak!

Nutritional Information		
2 Servings, each with:	22g Fat	9g Carbohydrate;
227 Calories;	(81.7% calories from fat);	3g Dietary Fiber;
	2g Protein;	6g Usable Carbs

Mortadella with Pesto Mayonnaise

Mortadella is like super-gourmet Italian bologna. Look for it in the best deli section you can find. The really good stuff has pistachios in it! This is good on a hot summer day.

Ingredients

2 teaspoons mayonnaise
(I use homemade)

½ teaspoon pesto sauce

1 ½ ounces mortadella
slices - about 3 slices

Instructions

1. Mix the mayo and pesto together.

2. Spread on the mortadella slices, roll up, and eat!

Nutritional Information Per Serving: 211 Calories; 20g Fat (83.3% calories from fat);	7g Protein; 1g Carbohydrate; trace Dietary Fiber; 1g Usable Carbs

Pepperoni Chips with Cream Cheese

I love these pepperoni chips! I think they'd be good crumbled over a salad, too.

Ingredients

1 ounce pepperoni slices

2 tablespoons whipped
cream cheese

Instructions

1. Lay your pepperoni slices on a microwaveable plate, and nuke them for 60 to 90 seconds, or until crisp.

2. Now eat them spread with the whipped cream cheese. That is all.

Nutritional Information
Per Serving:
211 Calories;
19g Fat
(83.7% calories from fat);
7g Protein;
2g Carbohydrate;
0g Dietary Fiber;
2g Usable Carbs

Cream Cheese Jalapeño Crunchies

The coconut oil takes this over the 80% fat mark. It's also very ketogenic.

Ingredients

2 tablespoons canned jalapeño pepper slices

Liquid sucralose to taste

1 teaspoon coconut oil

¼ cup whipped cream cheese

1/3 ounce pork rinds

Instructions

1. Mix the liquid sucralose with the peppers—I'd start with 3 to 4 drops. You want them hot, tangy, and sweet. Set aside while you...

2. Melt the coconut oil and stir it into the whipped cream cheese.

3. Be careful with your pork rinds; too many and you blow the fat ratio. Weigh them if you have a scale.

4. Now spread the pork rinds heavily with the cream cheese, add a slice or two of sweetened jalapeño, and chow 'em down! I love these.

Nutritional Information
Per Serving: 234 Calories;
22g Fat (82.7% calories from fat);
8g Protein;
2g Carbohydrate;
Trace Dietary Fiber;
2g Usable Carbs

Jalapeño Poppers

This makes one serving of two peppers, but you'll probably want to increase the recipe, or risk the family following you around, begging.

Ingredients

2 fresh jalapeño peppers

1 ½ ounces cream cheese

2 slices bacon

Instructions

1. Slit your peppers, remove the stems, and scrape out the seeds.

2. Divide the cream cheese into two chunks, and stuff each pepper with one.

3. Wrap each pepper with a slice of bacon, covering as completely as you can. Secure with toothpicks.

4. Wash your hands super-well with soap and water to get the hot pepper off!

5. Now broil or grill till the bacon is cooked. Devour!

Nutritional Information
Per Serving: 230 Calories;
21g Fat (82.3% calories from fat);
7g Protein;
3g Carbohydrate;
1g Dietary Fiber;
2g Usable Carbs

Fettuccini with Pancetta Cream

Wow. Just... wow.

Fettuccini with Pancetta Cream

Ingredients

1 packet tofu shirataki fettuccini

1 ounce pancetta (Italian bacon)

1 tablespoon butter

½ ounce cream cheese

1 teaspoon minced parsley

Nutritional Information
Per Serving: 207 Calories;
19g Fat
(81.4% calories from fat);
9g Protein;
1g Carbohydrate;
Trace Dietary Fiber;
1g Usable Carbs

Instructions

1. Drain and rinse your shirataki, and put them in a microwaveable bowl. Use your kitchen shears to snip across them a few times, then nuke 'em on high for two minutes, while you...

2. Chop the pancetta fairly fine. Put a medium-sized, heavy skillet over medium-low heat, and start the bits browning.

3. When the microwave beeps, drain the shirataki again, and nuke them for another minute. Go stir your pancetta!

4. You know the drill: when the microwave beeps again, drain the noodles again. Stir the pancetta!

5. Add the butter and cream cheese to the noodles, and toss till they're melted and have coated the noodles evenly.

6. Scrape the crispy pancetta bits and all the fat from the pan into the noodles. Toss again. Add the parsley, give it one last toss, and eat.

Blue Cheese Stuffed Celery

Ingredients

1 ½ ounces cream cheese

1 tablespoon heavy cream

1 tablespoon blue cheese, crumbled

½ clove garlic, crushed

Hot sauce to taste

2 large celery ribs

Instructions

1. Measure everything but the celery into a bowl, and use a fork to mash and stir it into a dip, leaving a few lumps of blue cheese.

2. Serve stuffed into the celery ribs.

Nutritional Information
Per Serving: 245 Calories;
23g Fat
(82.2% calories from fat);
6g Protein;
5g Carbohydrate;
1g Dietary Fiber;
4g Usable Carbs

Coleslaw

I love coleslaw, and this makes a nice big serving.

Ingredients

1 tablespoon sour cream

1 ½ tablespoons mayonnaise

½ teaspoon brown mustard

1 teaspoon cider vinegar

1 pinch Splenda or 1 drop liquid stevia extract

1 ½ cups shredded cabbage (You may use bagged coleslaw mix.)

Nutritional Information
Per Serving: 208 Calories;
21g Fat
(83.7% calories from fat);
2g Protein;
7g Carbohydrate;
2g Dietary Fiber;
5g Usable Carbs

Instructions

1. Mix together everything but the cabbage.

2. Pour over the cabbage and toss till evenly coated, then yum it down.

Coleslaw

Creamed Spinach

Simple!

Ingredients

10 ounces frozen chopped spinach

3 tablespoons butter

2 tablespoons cream cheese

Salt and pepper

Notes

Substitute Boursin for the cream cheese for a whole different flavor.

You'll get:

2 Servings,
each with: 246 Calories;
24g Fat
(82.6% calories from fat);
5g Protein;
6g Carbohydrate;
4g Dietary Fiber;
2g Usable Carbs

Instructions

1. Put your frozen spinach in a microwaveable casserole, add a couple of tablespoons of water, cover, and nuke on high for 8 minutes. When the microwave beeps, check to see if your spinach is done through. It'll probably still be a little cold in the middle - stir it up and give it another 3 to 4 minutes.

2. When your spinach is done, dump it in a strainer and press it hard with the back of a spoon to get out the excess water. Transfer to a bowl.

3. Stir in the butter and cream cheese, stirring till they're both melted and incorporated into a smooth sauce. Add salt and pepper to taste, divide into two servings, and eat.

4. If you're not sharing this, the second serving will reheat nicely in the microwave.

Creamed Spinach

Ham & Cheese Cups

Amy says: *I love quick, simple meals. This one is easy to throw together and very filling. It's become a new staple at our house.*

Ham & Cheese Cups

Ingredients

4 whole eggs

¾ cup heavy whipping cream

2 tablespoons butter, melted

½ cup ham, cubed

Salt and pepper, to taste

¾ cup shredded Monterey Jack cheese or pepper Jack cheese

Instructions

1. Beat the eggs, then mix in heavy cream and melted butter.

2. Stir in ham, salt, pepper, and shredded Monterey or pepper Jack cheese.

3. Pour into 6 sprayed muffin tins or ramekins, and cook at 400 degrees F for 25 to 30 minutes, or until knife inserted in the middle comes out clean.

Nutritional Information	
6 servings, each with:	10g Protein;
253 Calories;	2g Carbohydrate;
23g Fat	0g Dietary Fiber;
(82.1% calories from fat);	2g Usable Carbs

Curried Coconut Cream of Chicken Soup

Ingredients

1 teaspoon coconut oil

2 teaspoons curry powder

1 garlic clove, peeled and crushed

¾ cup coconut milk, unsweetened

1 cup chicken broth

1 teaspoon chicken bouillon concentrate

Instructions

1. In a small saucepan, over low heat, melt the coconut oil. Stir in the curry powder and sauté for a minute or two.

2. Add the garlic, coconut milk, chicken broth, and bouillon concentrate. Heat through, stirring to make sure the bouillon dissolves.

3. Let the whole thing simmer for five minutes, then serve.

Nutritional Information
2 Servings, each with:
217 Calories;
21g Fat
(83.8% calories from fat);
5g Protein;
5g Carbohydrate;
1g Dietary Fiber;
4g Usable Carbs

Garlicky Creamed Mushrooms

Half of this for you, as your whole feeding, the other half for a family member, served with a steak or chop.

Ingredients

8 ounces sliced mushrooms

2 ½ tablespoons butter

2 tablespoons Boursin cheese

Instructions

1. In your big, heavy skillet, over medium heat, sauté the mushrooms in the butter till they soften and change color.

2. Add the Boursin and stir till it melts. Serve.

Nutritional Information
2 Servings, each with:
215 Calories;
21g Fat
(83.9% calories from fat);
4g Protein;
6g Carbohydrate;
1g Dietary Fiber;
5g Usable Carbs

Notes

If you can't find Boursin (or Alouette, which is similar), you could use chive-and-onion cream cheese.

Salmon Bisque

Amy says: *My husband loves salmon. He also loves clam chowder. He declares this the best of both. I love the quick simplicity, as well as the taste.*

Ingredients

½ cup heavy cream

2 cups seafood stock

¼ cup canned salmon

1 teaspoon minced fresh dill weed

Salt and pepper

Instructions

1. Simply combine everything in a saucepan and bring to a simmer.

2. Let it cook for five minutes, then serve.

Nutritional Information
2 servings, each with:
245 Calories;
24g Fat
(86.1% calories from fat);
7g Protein;
2g Carbohydrate;
Trace Dietary Fiber;
2 g Usable Carbs

Notes:

The counts on this recipe were standardized using **Kitchen Basics** brand seafood stock; it's widely available in grocery stores, and can also be ordered through Amazon.com.

Salmon Bisque

Recipes 84% to 87% Fat

Not quite at that 90% ideal fat percentage, these recipes are still high enough to keep you in ketosis. Tasty, too!

Non-Recipes with 84% to 87% Fat

Pecans

1 ounce pecans (¼ cup) will have: 189 Calories; 19g Fat (85.4% calories from fat); 2g Protein; 5g Carbohydrate; 2g Dietary Fiber; 3g Usable Carbs

Olives

20 large olives marinated in 2 teaspoons olive oil will have: 181 Calories; 18g Fat (87.2% calories from fat); 1g Protein; 5g Carbohydrate; 3g Dietary Fiber; 2g Usable Carbs (You could just buy olives packed in olive oil, you know.)

Pate de foie gras

If you're feeling wealthy and have a really good gourmet food shop in the neighborhood, 1 ½ ounces pate de foie gras will have: 196 Calories; 19g Fat (86.0% calories from fat); 5g Protein; 2g Carbohydrate; 0g Dietary Fiber; 2g Usable Carbs

Fat Snacks

You'll think I've gone right 'round the bend, but I buy beef fat, cut it in strips, put it on my broiler rack, and bake it till it's crisp and brown. Then I salt it and eat it. I don't know the exact fat percentage here, because it will depend on how much fat cooks out of your, well, fat - there will actually be some protein in there, too. Still, this has served me well. Figure 1 ounce after cooking is a serving, and count it at 250 calories.

Non-Recipes with 84% to 87% Fat

Chocolate Peanut Butter Bombs

Amy says: *Fat bombs are becoming a popular way to increase fat while keeping carbs low. I've tried several recipes, but hadn't found one that really appealed to me. So I tweaked and reworked until this little gem was born.*

Servings 12

Ingredients

3 ounces 85% dark chocolate

8 tablespoons butter

3 tablespoons coconut oil

4 tablespoons natural creamy peanut butter

1 tablespoon heavy whipping cream

Sugar substitute equal to 6 teaspoons of sugar

½ cup macadamia nuts

Instructions

1. Melt chocolate and butter together in microwave. Add in rest of ingredients, except macadamia nuts, and mix until smooth.

2. Add macadamia nuts, stir, and pour into paper baking cups (about 2 to 3 teaspoons per cup).

3. Freeze until solid. Store in freezer.

4. Eat frozen or let them warm up for 5 minutes.

Nutritional Information	
12 servings, each with:	3g Protein;
209 Calories;	5g Carbohydrate;
21g Fat	2g Dietary Fiber;
(87.1% calories from fat);	3g Usable Carbs

Notes

Amy uses Lindt 85% dark chocolate for this recipe, and the counts are analyzed for that.

"Yogurt" Parfait

I've always loved yogurt with strawberries and nuts! This tastes much the same, but fits the Fat Fast parameters. Good on a hot summer morning.

Ingredients

1 tablespoon chopped pecans

1/3 cup sour cream

French vanilla liquid stevia

1 strawberry

Nutritional Information
Per Serving: 217 Calories;
21g Fat
(84.8% calories from fat);
3g Protein;
5g Carbohydrate;
1g Dietary Fiber;
4g Usable Carbs

Instructions

1. If you like, stir the chopped pecans in a small, heavy skillet over medium-low heat for a couple of minutes. This makes them crispier, and I like the flavor. Remove from heat.

2. In a smallish bowl, sweeten the sour cream to taste with the French vanilla liquid stevia - I find 6 to 8 drops about right. (If you'd prefer just a vanilla flavor with no sweetness, add a little vanilla extract instead.) Stir until evenly sweetened.

3. Slice or chop the strawberry. Top the sour cream with the strawberry and pecans, and eat.

"Yogurt" Parfait

Fat Fast Chicken Noodle Soup

Fat Fast Chicken Noodle Soup

Comfort food!

Ingredients

3 tablespoons coconut oil

2 tablespoons chopped onion

4 tablespoons diced celery

4 tablespoons shredded carrot

2 cups chicken broth

1 teaspoon chicken bouillon concentrate

1 package tofu shirataki (Fettuccini style is best for this)

Instructions

1. In a medium saucepan over medium-low heat, melt the coconut oil. Add the vegetables and sauté for five minutes or so.

2. Add the chicken broth and bouillon concentrate and bring to a simmer. Cover, reduce heat to low, and let it simmer for 20 minutes or so, till the veggies are soft.

3. Meanwhile, drain and rinse the shirataki noodles. Put 'em in a microwaveable bowl and nuke on high for 2 minutes, then drain again. Snip across them a few times with your kitchen shears.

4. When the veggies are soft, add the noodles to the soup. Let it simmer another minute or so, and eat.

Nutritional Information	22g Fat	4g Carbohydrate;
2 Servings, each with:	(84.0% calories from fat);	1g Dietary Fiber;
230 Calories;	5g Protein;	3g Usable Carbs

Pumpkin Pie "Cheesecake"

The family will like this, too.

Ingredients

10 tablespoons pumpkin puree

8 ounces cream cheese, softened

1 teaspoon pumpkin pie spice

15 drops liquid stevia extract

3 tablespoons heavy cream

Instructions

1. Easy! Just use an electric mixer to beat everything together till it's fluffy.

2. Divide into four dishes and chill before serving.

Nutritional Information
4 Servings, each with:
251 Calories;
24g Fat
(84.2% calories from fat);
5g Protein;
5g Carbohydrate;
1g Dietary Fiber;
4g Usable Carbs

Asparagus with Wasabi Mayonnaise

Ingredients

½ pound asparagus

2 tablespoons mayonnaise

¼ teaspoon wasabi powder

¼ teaspoon soy sauce or coconut aminos

1 pinch Splenda

Nutritional Information
Per Serving: 226 Calories;
24g Fat

(85.9% calories from fat);
3g Protein;
6g Carbohydrate;
2g Dietary Fiber;
4g Usable Carbs

Instructions

1. Snap the ends off your asparagus where it wants to break naturally.

2. Put in a microwave steamer or lay it in a microwaveable casserole or pie plate.

3. Add a tablespoon or so of water, cover (use plastic wrap if you don't have a lid), and microwave on high for 3 to 4 minutes.

4. Stir everything else together in a small dish.

5. When the microwave beeps, uncover your asparagus immediately, to avoid overcooking.

6. Now you have a choice: You can eat your asparagus immediately, dipping it in the mayo, or you can chill it and eat it later. Good either way.

Notes

Coconut Aminos are very similar to soy sauce, and a great alternative for those who are avoiding all soy. Get them at your local health food store, or online.

Asparagus with Chipotle Mayonnaise

This makes four servings for the simple reason that it's rough to subdivide the pepper and run so little mayo through the food processor. But feel free to make the mayo first, keep it in the fridge, and nuke the asparagus as needed.

Ingredients

2 pounds asparagus

½ cup mayonnaise

1 chipotle chili, canned in adobo

Nutritional Information

4 Servings, each with:
225 Calories;
24g Fat
(85.9% calories from fat);
3g Protein;
5g Carbohydrate;
3g Dietary Fiber;
2g Usable Carbs

Instructions

1. Snap the ends off the asparagus where they want to break naturally. Put in a microwaveable casserole or Pyrex baking pan, add a couple of tablespoons of water, cover with plastic wrap, and nuke on high for 6 minutes.

2. In the meanwhile, put the mayonnaise and the chipotle in your food processor, with the S-blade in place. Add a teaspoon of the adobo sauce from the can. Now, run the food processor until it's smooth. That's it.

3. Serve ¼ of the asparagus with 2 tablespoons chipotle mayonnaise.

Asparagus with Chipotle Mayonnaise

Spinach Salad

Ingredients

1 ½ cups fresh spinach

4 teaspoons olive oil

4 teaspoons cider vinegar

½ teaspoon no-sugar-added ketchup (Heinz makes a good one)

1 fresh mushroom, sliced

1 slice cooked bacon, crumbled

Instructions

1. Measure your spinach and put it in a salad bowl.

2. Whisk together the olive oil, vinegar, and ketchup, pour over the spinach, and toss well.

3. Top with the sliced mushroom, crumble in the bacon, and eat.

Nutritional Information	
1 serving with: 215 Calories;	4g Protein;
21g Fat	4g Carbohydrate;
(85.9% calories from fat);	1g Dietary Fiber;
	3g Usable Carbs

Spinach Salad

Pumpkin Pies

Amy says: *My husband loves these individual pumpkin pies; this is one of the many reasons he looks forward to autumn.*

Ingredients

- 15-ounce can pumpkin puree, 100% pure pumpkin

- 4 ounces cream cheese, softened

- 2 whole eggs, beaten

- ½ teaspoon pumpkin pie spice

- ½ cup heavy whipping cream

- Sugar-free sweetener to equal ¼ cup sugar

- 2 tablespoons of whipped cream, optional garnish

Instructions

1. Preheat oven to 350 degrees F.

2. Using an electric mixer, beat pumpkin and cream cheese until smooth.

3. Beat in the eggs, pumpkin pie spice, heavy cream, and sweetener.

4. Pour into greased ramekins, placed on a cookie sheet. Bake for 60 minutes, or until knife inserted in center comes out clean.

5. Cool and serve, or refrigerate until ready to eat.

Nutritional Information	
6 servings, each with	4g Protein;
162 Calories;	3g Carbohydrate;
15g Fat	Trace Dietary Fiber;
(84.3% calories from fat);	3g Usable Carbs

(Dana's Note: 2 tablespoons of whipped cream - measured after whipping, not before - as a topping will add 52 calories and 6 grams of fat, for a calorie count of 214, and 88% fat.)

Pumpkin Pies

Fat Fast Mac-and-Cheese / Lemony Cream Cheese

Fat Fast Mac-and-Cheese

The crowning glory of this book. You'll make this over and over, whether you're Fat Fasting or not. A little high in calories, but worth giving up another feeding for!

Ingredients

1 packet tofu shirataki (I like the macaroni-style best for this.)

2 tablespoons heavy cream

1 tablespoon whipped cream cheese

1 ¼ ounces Cheddar cheese, shredded

½ tablespoon coconut oil

Instructions

1. Drain and rinse 1 packet of tofu shirataki - I like the Fettuccini width or the hard-to-find macaroni shape for this.

2. Put 'em in a bowl, and nuke them on high for 90 seconds or so.

3. Drain them again. Nuke them again. Drain them again. This should get the excess water out.

4. Add everything else to the bowl, and stir till the cheese melts and you have a smooth sauce. That's all!

Nutritional Information		
Per Serving: 339 Calories;	(86.4% calories from fat);	Trace Dietary Fiber;
33g Fat	10g Protein;	2g Usable Carbs
	2g Carbohydrate;	

Lemony Cream Cheese

Rebecca says: *Dr. Atkins recommended plain cream cheese when doing a fat fast, and when I first tried it years ago, I realized how yummy it was. I tried different things to make it even yummier and came up with this version, which is my favorite.*

Ingredients

2 ounces cream cheese, at room temperature

2 teaspoon bottled or fresh organic lemon juice

4 drops stevia extract, unflavored

Instructions

1. Put all ingredients into a small bowl and mix until well blended. Enjoy!

Dana's Note: 2 tablespoons of whipped cream – measured after whipping, not before – as a topping will add 52 calories and 6 grams of fat, for a calorie count of 214, and 88% fat.

Nutritional Information		
1 serving with:	19.6g Fat	2.4g Carbs,
203 Calories,	(86.9% calories from fat),	0g Fiber,
	4.2g Protein,	2.4g Usable Carbs

Chocolate Cheese Mousse

Decadent, cheesecake-like flavor without all the work.
Two servings of about 5 tablespoons each.

Ingredients

½ ounce unsweetened
  baking chocolate

¼ cup sour cream

1/3 cup whipped cream
  cheese

15 drops chocolate stevia

5 drops French vanilla
  stevia

Instructions

1. Put the chocolate in a bowl, and microwave for 1 minute. See if it's melted; if not give it another 30 seconds.

2. When the chocolate is melted, add everything else. Stir up really well, until there are no streaks of bitter chocolate left.

Nutritional Information	19g Fat	4g Carbohydrate;
2 Servings, each with:	(85.6% calories from fat);	1g Dietary Fiber;
192 Calories;	3g Protein;	3g Usable Carbs

Curried Cream of Chicken Soup

You'll notice a certain similarity, here, to the Curried Coconut Cream of Chicken Soup. We figured some of you might not be able to buy coconut milk locally. And anyway, this is a little higher in fat.

Ingredients

2 teaspoons coconut oil or
  butter

2 teaspoons curry powder

1/3 cup heavy cream

1 cup chicken broth

1 teaspoon coconut oil

1 garlic clove, peeled and
  crushed

1 teaspoon chicken bouillon
  granules

Instructions

1. In a small saucepan over low heat, melt the coconut oil. Stir in the curry powder, and sauté for a minute or two.

2. Add everything else, and bring to a simmer, stirring to make sure the bouillon concentrate dissolves.

3. Simmer for five minutes or so, then serve.

Nutritional Information	4g Protein;
2 Servings, each with:	3g Carbohydrate;
226 Calories;	1g Dietary Fiber;
23g Fat	2g Usable Carbs
(87.6% calories from fat);	

Butter-Roasted Pecans

Be careful! It is SO easy to blow past the ¼ cup serving size with these. I recommend that you measure these out into single portions and put in zipper-lock bags as soon as they're cool.

Ingredients

3 tablespoons butter

2 cups pecan halves

Salt if desired

Nutritional Information
8 Servings, each with:
218 Calories;
23g Fat
(87.8% calories from fat);
2g Protein;
5g Carbohydrate;
2g Dietary Fiber;
3g Usable Carbs

Instructions

1. Preheat oven to 350 degrees F. Put a roasting pan in the oven to warm.

2. Pull your warm pan out of the oven and melt the butter in the bottom. Now add the pecans, and stir quite a, until they're evenly coated.

3. Roast for 4 minutes (set the timer), then stir. Roast for another 4 to 5 minutes, then remove from oven. Sprinkle with salt, if desired, then cool and portion out by the ¼ cup into individual bags.

Notes

For a nice variation, use seasoned salt or Creole or Cajun seasoning.

Make these with coconut oil instead of butter for extra ketosis power.

8 Servings, each with: 224 Calories; 23g Fat (88.2% calories from fat); 2g Protein; 5g Carbohydrate; 2g Dietary Fiber; 3g Usable Carbs

Butter-Roasted Pecans

Curried Pecans

You may well find yourself making these for parties, they're so good.

Ingredients

3 tablespoons coconut oil

1 teaspoon curry powder

¼ teaspoon garlic powder

½ teaspoon onion powder

8 ounces pecans

Salt to taste

Nutritional Information
8 Servings,
each with: 235 Calories;
24g Fat
(87.6% calories from fat);
2g Protein;
5g Carbohydrate;
2g Dietary Fiber;
3g Usable Carbs

Instructions

1. Preheat your oven to 350 degrees F. Put the coconut oil in a roasting pan, and slide it into the oven while it heats.

2. When the coconut oil is melted, pull pan out of the oven and stir in the seasonings. Now add the pecans and stir really well, till they're all evenly coated.

3. Roast for 5 minutes. Stir, then roast for another 4 to 5 minutes. Cool, salt to taste, then divide into ¼ cup portions, and put into individual zipper-lock bags.

Curried Pecans

Mexican Hot Chocolate

Chocolate, cinnamon, and vanilla are a traditional Mexican combination, and with good reason. I made this with coconut milk for all you folks who are avoiding dairy.

Ingredients

½ cup coconut milk, unsweetened

¼ cup water

2 teaspoons cocoa powder

¼ teaspoon cinnamon

12 drops French vanilla stevia, or to taste

Instructions

1. Simply whisk everything together in a mug till the cocoa power and cinnamon are completely blended in.

2. Microwave till hot. Give it one more stir, and sip.

Nutritional Information
Per Serving: 231 Calories;
24g Fat
(86.7% calories from fat);
3g Protein;
5g Carbohydrate;
1g Dietary Fiber;
4g Usable Carbs

Mexican Hot Chocolate

Recipes 88% Fat and Up

Here you will find the super-high-fat recipes - 88% of calories or more from fat. The more you choose from this chapter, the deeper into ketosis you're likely to go. Too, these recipes will help balance out the lower fat recipes in the earlier chapters. But remember: Fat Fasting is about super-high-fat *and* calorie restriction, both, so watch your portions.

Non-Recipes 88% Fat and Up

Macadamia Nuts

1 ounce macadamia nuts (¼ cup) will have: 199 Calories; 21g Fat (88.3% calories from fat); 2g Protein; 4g Carbohydrate; 3g Dietary Fiber; 1g Usable Carbs

Cream Cheese

2 ounces cream cheese will have: 198 Calories; 20g Fat (88.5% calories from fat); 4g Protein; 2g Carbohydrate; 0g Dietary Fiber; 2g Usable Carbs

Sugar Free Gelatin with Heavy Cream

1 serving prepared sugar-free, gelatin dessert with ¼ cup of heavy cream, whipped, will have: 214 Calories; 22g Fat (90.7% calories from fat); 3g Protein; 2g Carbohydrate; 0g Dietary Fiber; 2g Usable Carbs

Non-Recipes 88% Fat and Up

Coco Cocoa Fat Bombs

Rebecca says: *There are lots of recipes floating around for fat bombs, and this one is my contribution to the growing collection. I enjoy one of these candies just as much as a good piece of dark chocolate. I keep them in the freezer because they melt pretty quickly when I hold them in my hot little fingers!*

Ingredients

2 teaspoons coconut oil, melted

2 teaspoons salted butter, melted

2 teaspoons 100% almond butter

3/8 teaspoon unsweetened cocoa powder

5 drops stevia extract, flavored or unflavored

Instructions

1. Put all ingredients into a small bowl and stir until well mixed. At this point, you can pour the candy into a mini cupcake paper and freeze it for 15 to 20 minutes, or you can just freeze it right in the bowl. Obviously, if you are making a batch of 20 or so, you will want to line up cupcake papers on a baking sheet and evenly divide the candy mixture into them.

2. After freezing, you can store them together in an airtight container in the freezer.

3. Eat frozen or let thaw for 5 minutes.

Nutritional Information	22.7g Fat	2.8g Carbohydrate;
1 serving with:	(90.5% calories from fat),	2g Fiber,
225 Calories,	2.6g Protein,	0.8g Usable Carbs

Chocolate Whip

Turns heavy cream into an indulgent dish of chocolaty goodness.

Ingredients

½ cup heavy cream, chilled

1 tablespoon cocoa powder

5 drops chocolate liquid stevia

5 drops French vanilla liquid stevia

Instructions

1. Simple: Using your electric mixer (not a blender or food processor), whip everything together until the cream is stiff. Don't over-beat, or you'll get chocolate butter!

2. Divide into two dishes. If you're saving one for later (instead of sharing with someone), cover it with plastic wrap before refrigerating.

Nutritional Information
2 Servings,
each with: 211 Calories;
22g Fat
(91.2% calories from fat);
2g Protein;
3g Carbohydrate;
1g Dietary Fiber;
2g Usable Carbs

Chocolate Whip

Coconut Flax Bread

Grain-free, gluten-free, and delicious! Buttered toast is a staple again in my house.

Coconut Flax Bread

ngredients

4 cups shredded coconut meat

¾ cup flax seed meal

1 tablespoon xanthan

1 teaspoon erythritol (Not essential, but I think it improves the flavor. You could use another sweetener to equal 1 teaspoon sugar if you prefer.)

1 ½ teaspoons baking soda

½ teaspoon salt

½ cup water

2 tablespoons cider vinegar

4 eggs

Nutritional Information
20 slices,
each with: 111 Calories;
9g Fat
(69.9% calories from fat);
4g Protein;
5g Carbohydrate;
4g Dietary Fiber;
37mg Cholesterol;
165mg Sodium,
1g Usable Carbs

Instructions

1. Preheat oven to 350 degrees F. Grease a loaf pan - standard, not super-huge; the opening on mine is 8 ½" x 4 ½". Now line it - or at least the bottom - with non-stick aluminum foil or baking parchment.

2. In your food processor, with the S-blade in place, combine the coconut, flax seed meal, xanthan, erythritol, baking soda, and salt. Run the processor till everything is ground to a fine meal. Scrape down the sides and run the processor some more. You want it all quite fine.

3. While that's happening, in a glass measuring cup, combine the water and the vinegar. Have this standing by the food processor.

4. While the food processor is running, add the eggs, one at a time, through the feed tube. Let each one be completely incorporated before adding the next. If you have to stop the processor and scrape down the sides to get this to happen, do it. You want the dough evenly mixed.

5. Finally, pour the water and vinegar mixture in through the feed tube. Run just until everything is evenly combined - again, scrape down the sides if needed.

6. Pour/scrape the batter into the prepared loaf pan. Smooth the top. Bake for 1 hour and 15 minutes. Turn out on a wire rack to cool.

7. This slices beautifully, and can be sliced thick or thin. I get about 20 slices per loaf, so that's what I calculated on.

Coconut Flax Bread

Notes

You'll notice that the fat percentage on this is too low. That's where butter comes in! Add two teaspoons of butter - toasting first is optional - and you're up to 179 calories, and 17 grams of fat. That's 85% fat! Or you can add 1 teaspoon of butter and 1 tablespoon of cream cheese, for 195 calories, 17 grams fat. That's only 78% fat, but it should be okay.

I originally made this bread with coconut butter I had made myself, from the recipe in this book. Then I had the idea of just grinding the coconut with all the other dry ingredients, which seemed far simpler. It was, and it worked fine. If you buy it in bulk - it's worth looking for! - shredded coconut is quite cheap; I pay $3/pound.

These measurements assume finely shredded coconut. If all you can find is flaked coconut, you'll need to weigh it instead of measuring by volume. My four cups of shredded coconut weighed 9.5 ounces.

And for the love of all that's holy, do not buy sweetened "angel" or "macaroon" coconut!!

Regarding food processors: This is a snap in my professional-quality Cuisinart. However, some of you may not have a machine that powerful. Some of you may not have a food processor at all, and not have $150-200 to invest. Therefore, I tried making this in my $30 Black and Decker food processor. It handled the grinding process pretty well, though I did have to stop the machine and scrape down the sides and around the bottom edge a couple of times. It bogged down, however, on incorporating the eggs. After each egg was added, I had to take the lid off and use a spoon - this worked better than a rubber scraper - to scrape down the sides, all the way down to the bottom edge, making sure that everything got evenly mixed. Ditto when I added the water and vinegar. Still, it worked, and turned out a perfectly nice loaf of bread. And if you look at the price of commercially-produced grain-free bread, you'll find that $30 is a comparatively modest investment. That said, if you can afford it, go for the Cuisinart.

Regarding the xanthan gum: You can use guar gum or glucomannan powder in place of the xanthan gum, but I think the xanthan gum works best. Don't skip this, by the way; the bread is dreadfully crumbly without it.

Fettuccini Alfredo

Simple and very satisfying.

Ingredients

1 packet tofu shirataki (fettuccini style, of course!)

1 tablespoon cream cheese with chives and onions

1 tablespoon butter

2 tablespoons grated Romano or Parmesan cheese

Instructions

1. Drain and rinse your shirataki, and put 'em in a microwaveable bowl. Nuke on high for two minutes, and drain again. Nuke for another minute and drain one more time. Return to the bowl.

2. Add the chive-and-onion cream cheese and butter, and stir till they melt to combine into a smooth sauce.

3. Sprinkle with 1 tablespoon of the Romano or Parmesan and stir in. Top with the last tablespoon of cheese, and eat.

Nutritional Information	19g Fat	1g Carbohydrate;
1 serving with:	(87.5% calories from fat);	trace Dietary Fiber;
191 Calories;	5g Protein;	1g Usable Carbs

Fettuccini Alfredo

Fettuccini with Pesto

My adorable neighbor Keith Johnson, of _Permaculture Activist_, asked me to harvest his basil while he was out of town for two weeks. I made a whole lot of pesto with it. I gave most of it to him, but kept a container for myself - and made this.

Ingredients

1 packet tofu shirataki

1 tablespoon pesto sauce

1 tablespoon olive oil

Instructions

1. By now you know the drill: Drain and rinse the noodles, nuke for two minutes, drain again, nuke for another minute, drain one more time. Snip across 'em with your shears.

2. Now add the olive oil and pesto, and toss till everything's evenly distributed. Eat!

Nutritional Information	21g Fat	1g Carbohydrate;
1 serving with:	(92.8% calories from fat);	trace Dietary Fiber;
195 Calories;	2g Protein;	1g Usable Carbs

Fettuccini with Pesto

Sautéed Mushrooms

When you're done Fat Fasting, try these over a steak!

Ingredients

3 ounces mushrooms

1 tablespoon olive oil

1 tablespoon butter

¼ teaspoon onion powder

¼ teaspoon garlic powder

Salt and pepper

Instructions

1. If your mushrooms aren't sliced, slice 'em. (I buy mine sliced.)

2. Over medium heat, combine the olive oil and butter in a medium-sized skillet. Add the onion and garlic powder and stir.

3. Now sauté the mushrooms until they've softened and changed color. Sprinkle with salt and pepper to taste, and eat.

Nutritional Information	25g Fat	5g Carbohydrate;
Per Serving:	(89.4% calories from fat);	1g Dietary Fiber; 4g Usable
246 Calories;	2g Protein;	Carbs

Sautéed Mushrooms

Sweet-and-Tangy Macaroni Salad

Not only is this delicious, it's one of the most filling recipes in this book.

Ingredients

1 packet tofu shirataki, macaroni style

1 ½ tablespoons roasted red bell pepper

1 ½ tablespoons chopped sugar-free bread-and-butter pickles

2 tablespoons diced celery

1 ½ tablespoons sliced scallion

1 ½ tablespoons chopped black olives

2 tablespoons mayonnaise

½ teaspoon red wine vinegar

½ teaspoon pickle juice

2 dashes hot sauce, or to taste

Salt and pepper

Instructions

1. Drain and rinse your shirataki and put 'em in a bowl. Microwave on high for two minutes, then drain again. Repeat - nuke and drain again. Leave them in the strainer to cool while you...

2. Chop your roasted red pepper, sugar-free bread-and-butter pickles, and celery, and slice your scallions thin, including the crisp part of the green shoot. Yes, put a tablespoon on your cutting board and measure all these things. Tedious, I know, but fat-fasting is about precision. Put all this stuff in a bowl as it's chopped. I'm assuming you bought chopped ripe olives - you can get a little can of them in any grocery store - so measure in your 1 ½ tablespoons of olives, as well. (If you didn't buy 'em chopped, you'll want to chop them first, of course.)

3. Okay, noodles are cool. Dump 'em in with the chopped veggies. Measure in the mayo, vinegar, juice from the sugar-free bread-and-butter pickles, and hot sauce. Stir until everything is evenly mixed and coated with dressing. Add salt and pepper to taste.

4. If you can stand the delay, this will improve with a few hours of chilling. But I've been known to eat it straight out of the mixing bowl as soon as it was done, and never regretted it.

Nutritional Information	25g Fat	3g Carbohydrate;
Per Serving:	(93.8% calories from fat);	1g Dietary Fiber;
223 Calories;	1g Protein;	2g Usable Carbs

Sweet-and-Tangy Macaroni Salad

Mocha Mascarpone Mousse

Mocha Mascarpone Mousse

This makes six servings, so be sure you want to eat mousse a lot for a couple of days, or share it with your family. I'm afraid halving the recipe doesn't work, because of that one egg yolk.

Ingredients

½ cup heavy cream, chilled

8 ounces mascarpone cheese

1 egg yolk

¼ cup chocolate flavored sugar-free syrup

2 teaspoons instant coffee

1 teaspoon vanilla extract

1 ½ teaspoons cocoa powder

Instructions

1. In a deep, narrow bowl, using an electric mixer, whip the cream until stiff. Set aside while you...
2. Use your mixer to whip together the mascarpone, egg yolk, chocolate flavored sugar-free syrup, instant coffee, and vanilla. Whip, scraping down the sides of the bowl from time to time, for a good 2 to 3 minutes.
3. Using a rubber scraper, gently but thoroughly fold the whipped cream into the mascarpone mixture. Divide into small dishes - remember, this is to be 6 servings - and dust lightly with cocoa powder.
4. Chill well before serving.

Nutritional Information

Per Serving: 252 Calories;
26g Fat
(91.2% calories from fat);
3g Protein;
3g Carbohydrate;
trace Dietary Fiber;
3g Usable Carbs

Notes

Again, I am not afraid of raw eggs, but if you're wary of them, look for pasteurized eggs.

Rise and Shine Cocktail

Rebecca says: *This is the first thing I eat in the morning. Not only is it a good start to a Fat Fasting day, but it has the added benefit of being a liver cleanse and detox, according to some low-carb writers. If you are new to coconut oil or MCT oil, you may need to start with less if your tummy gets upset. As you adjust to the oil, you can increase it until you reach the amounts in this recipe.*

Ingredients

1 tablespoon extra-virgin olive oil

1 tablespoon coconut oil (melted) or MCT oil or liquid coconut oil

1 tablespoon fresh or bottled organic lemon juice

5 drops unflavored liquid stevia extract

Instructions

1. Put all ingredients into a small cup or jar with a tight lid and shake for 30 seconds.
2. Drink up!

Nutritional Information

1 serving with: 257 calories;
27.9 grams fat
98% calories from fat;
0.1g protein;
1g Carbohydrate;
trace Fiber;
0g Usable Carbs

Keto Coffee

This Paleo/low carb-friendly coffee - with unsalted butter instead of cream - is gaining popularity, but coconut oil is more ketogenic than butter. That Nice Boy I Married loved this, said it was better than coffee with regular cream.

Ingredients

1 cup hot brewed coffee

2 tablespoons coconut milk, unsweetened

1 tablespoon coconut oil

1 ½ teaspoons vanilla flavored sugar-free syrup

Instructions

This is simple: Just combine everything in your blender and run until the coconut milk has melted and it's frothy.

Nutritional Information

1 serving,
with: 178 Calories; 20g Fat
94.7% calories from fat;
1g Protein;
2g Carbohydrate;
0g Dietary Fiber;
2g Usable Carbs

Notes

Feel free to substitute vanilla extract and the sweetener of your choice for the vanilla flavored sugar-free syrup, or you could try French vanilla liquid stevia extract.

Caramel Coffee

Simple, tasty, and makes a nice treat first thing in the morning.

Ingredients

1 cup hot coffee

¼ cup heavy whipping cream

1 tablespoon caramel flavored sugar-free syrup

Instructions

Brew coffee, mix in syrup and heavy cream, and stir well.

Nutritional Information

1 serving, with: 210 Calories; 22g Fat (92.4% calories from fat); 1g Protein; 3g Carbohydrate; 0g Dietary Fiber; 3 g Usable Carbs

Notes

Feel free to substitute your favorite flavored sugar-free syrup - chocolate would be good here, or hazelnut.

Caramel Coffee

French Vanilla Iced Coffee

If you make the coffee the night before and stash it in the fridge, you can make this in no time for a cool and quick breakfast.

French Vanilla Iced Coffee

Ingredients

½ cup coconut milk, unsweetened

½ cup brewed coffee, chilled

18 drops French vanilla liquid stevia

3 ice cubes

Instructions

Put the coconut milk, coffee, and stevia in your blender.

Turn it on, and add ice cubes, one at a time, blending until they're crushed. Pour into a glass and drink.

Nutritional Information
Per Serving: 224 Calories;
24g Fat
90.2% calories from fat;
2g Protein;
3g Carbohydrate;
0g Dietary Fiber;
3g Usable Carbs

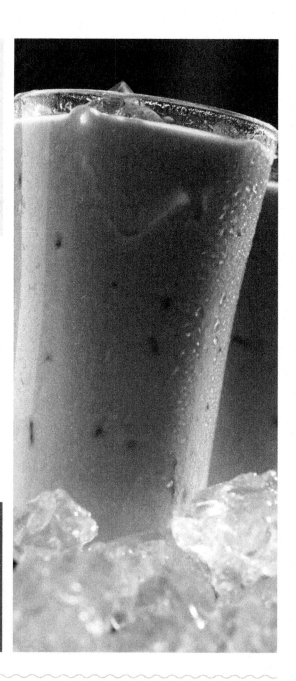

Acknowledgements

The Fat Fast Cookbook is the result of many dedicated low carb dieters trying to help the low carb community break their weight loss plateaus. Without Dr. Robert C. Atkins, most of us would probably still be eating the foods in MyPlate (formerly known as the food pyramid) in the quantities the U.S. Department of Agriculture tells us to eat. (And why is it the U.S. Department of Agriculture dictating our food choices instead of the U.S. Department of Health and Human Services or some other qualified organization?) Marcy Guyer managed the writing of the cookbook and organized the team. Azure Zebra Productions created the cover design using an Amy Dungan photograph. Interior page layout created by John Furkin from Prospect House Designs. Judy Barnes Baker proofread the document and guided us through the production phase.

Resources

www.fatfastrecipes.com/resources

FatFastRecipes.com - The home of the Fat Fast Cookbook
and the largest collection of information related to the
Fat Fast. Here you'll find free Fat Fast recipes, a list of
ingredients for making your Fat Fast recipes, the PDF
version of the Fat Fast Cookbook, and other resources.

Purchase Fat Fast Cookbook as a paperback, eBook, or
downloadable PDF version at FatFastRecipes.com

FREE Bonus PDF Files For Fat Fast Cookbook:
Bonus Recipes for Fat Fast Cookbook
- 5 extra high fat recipes to help you do the Fat Fast.

Top 10 Low Carb Articles from CarbSmart.com
- CarbSmart.com has been your trusted guide to the
low carb lifestyle since 1999. We've published over 2,200
articles to help you live a better life including these Top 10.

Fat Fast Shopping Guide
- A list of popular ingredients you can purchase
from Amazon.com or your local grocery store to help you do
the Fat Fast.

Ingredients for Fat Fast Recipes at Amazon.com
- We've made it easy for you to purchase all the ingredients
you need for your Fat Fast recipes from Amazon.com.

Dana Carpender's Page on Amazon.com
- We've made it easy for you to purchase all of Dana's books
from Amazon.com.

CarbSmart.com - CarbSmart is the publisher of Fat Fast Cookbook and the web site CarbSmart.com is your trusted guide to the low-carb lifestyle. Since 1999, we've published the latest news, information, product reviews, and success stories to help you succeed at your low-carb lifestyle.
Visit us at www.CarbSmart.com

GlutenSmart.com - GlutenSmart is the sister website to CarbSmart focusing on the needs of the Celiac and gluten-free community and will soon be publishing it's own series of gluten-free cookbooks.
Visit us at www.GlutenSmart.com.

HoldTheToast.com - The web site of Dana Carpender, the author of Fat Fast Cookbook. Dana has been publishing her perspective on the low-carb lifestyle since 1999.

HealthyLowCarbLiving.com - The (low-carb) web site of Amy Dungan, contributor to the Fat Fast Cookbook.

My Low Carb Road to Better Health - The web site of Rebecca Latham, contributor to the Fat Fast Cookbook.

Amy Dungan Photography - The (photography) web site of Amy Dungan, contributor to the Fat Fast Cookbook.

Guyer Photography - The web site of Jeff Guyer, photographic contributor to the Fat Fast Cookbook. Guyer Photography specializes in weddings and special events, as well as portrait, fine art, and architectural photography.

Resources

Resources

CarbSmart Magazine

CarbSmart also publishes a <u>digital magazine</u> available in the <u>Apple iTunes Newsstand</u> and as a <u>downloadable PDF file</u>.

CarbSmart Magazine is a monthly publication that supports the low carb community and helps educate both newbies and experienced low carbers.

Despite the many diets and exercise programs now available, obesity is not beating a retreat. Instead, it is on the rise: 36 percent of the U.S. population today is considered obese compared with only 28 percent when CarbSmart.com first started publishing online in 1999.

Type 2 diabetes is also increasing at alarming rates. In the U.S,. more than 11 percent of adults, as well as one in every 400 children and more than 25 percent of seniors are diabetic. Another 35 percent of the U.S. population is at risk for diabetes and rates of diabetes and obesity are rising worldwide.

CarbSmart Magazine brings news of the low carb, diabetic, and Paleo lifestyles to all who can benefit from them – and we believe that's just about everyone.

Best selling author Dana Carpender, who has written 17 books, including her two latest, 500 Paleo Recipes and The Fat Fast Cookbook, is the managing editor. "CarbSmart Magazine provides up-to-date and unbiased information about the many benefits of the low carb lifestyle," says Carpender. "Our focus is to cover anything that will help our readers be successful on a low carb diet, so they can reap its many benefits. We also provide information about low carb diets to control or eliminate diabetes. And we evaluate and report on the latest research & information about carbohydrate restriction and diabetic and Paleo diets to help our readers understand how these diets may help them." CarbSmart Magazine also contains product and restaurant reviews, as well as practical tips on everything from family meal planning to eating on the go. The magazine's goal is to help its readers incorporate healthy living into every aspect of their daily lives. Our team includes some of the best-known writers in the low carb community, plus some up-and-comers: Jimmy Moore, Dr. James Carlson, Jacqueline Eberstein RN, Amy Dungan, Susie T. Gibbs, Caitlin Weeks, Tara Grant, Fred Hahn, and many more.

About the Authors

Dana Carpender

A pioneer of the low carb frontier, best-selling author Dana Carpender went low carb in 1995, after whole-grain-and-beaning her way up to a size 20. Immediate weight loss and sky-rocketing energy told her this was what her body had been waiting for her to do, that she had set her foot on a path from which there was no return. However, it rapidly became clear that to eat this way for life, she - and others - needed the answer to one simple question: What's for dinner? The answer will be found in her cookbooks, eleven of them so far, encompassing over 2,500 recipes. Dana has been fighting the low-fat lie since 1998 at <u>HoldTheToast.com</u>. She lives in Indiana with three dogs, a cat, a backyard full of chickens - and, of course, That Nice Boy She Married, with whom she shares much bacon on a pleasant Sunday morning.

Amy Dungan

Amy is a writer and photographer, living in Southern Illinois with her husband and two children. She started on the low-carb lifestyle in 2001 after frantically searching for a way to lose weight and deal with health problems. She's had some ups and downs over the years, but continues to push forward in the pursuit of good health. In her free time, she enjoys embarrassing her kids in public, spending time with her husband, and contemplating the true meaning of bacon. You can learn more about her continuing journey at healthylowcarbliving.com.

Rebecca Latham

Rebecca started the low-carb lifestyle in 2009 after trying to lose weight the conventional way - low-fat and high-carb. After her initial success on Atkins (her story can be found in The New Atkins For a New You), Rebecca found that something else was needed to lose the remaining weight and keep it off. Lowering protein and raising fat has done the trick. Rebecca has reached her goal weight and is maintaining very nicely! She runs a long arm quilting business out of her home where her customers take home quilts that sometimes smell suspiciously like bacon. You can read more about how she eats at lowcarbbetterhealth.blogspot.com.

About the Authors

CPSIA information can be obtained
at www.ICGtesting.com
Printed in the USA
LVOW05s2257020616

491033LV00009BA/130/P